10 South Dod

THE RENAISSANCE

Medieval or Modern?

esoteric

assize

demographic

PROBLEMS IN EUROPEAN CIVILIZATION

UNDER THE EDITORIAL DIRECTION OF

Ralph W. Greenlaw* and Dwight E. Lee†

Other volumes in preparation

PROBLEMS IN EUROPEAN CIVILIZATION

THE
RENAISSANCE

Medieval or Modern?

EDITED WITH AN INTRODUCTION BY

Karl H. Dannenfeldt, ARIZONA STATE UNIVERSITY

D. C. HEATH AND COMPANY · BOSTON

Library of Congress Catalog Card number 59-8438

Table of Contents

Introduction

In 1860 in the introduction to his work on *The Civilization of the Renaissance in Italy*, Jacob Burckhardt predicted the present "Problem of the Renaissance" when he wrote "To each eye, perhaps, the outlines of a great civilization present a different picture. . . . In the wide ocean upon which we venture, the possible ways and directions are many; and the same studies which have served for this work might easily, in other hands, not only receive a wholly different treatment and application, but lead to essentially different conclusions."

To the writers of the Italian Renaissance itself, there was no serious problem. Their views of the age in which they were living furnished the basis for a long-held concept, namely, that after a period of about a thousand years of cultural darkness and ignorance, there arose a new age with a great revival in classical literature, learning, and the arts.

The humanists of the Northern Renaissance continued this concept. "Out of the thick Gothic night our eyes are opened to the glorious torch of the sun," wrote Rabelais. Moreover, there was also now introduced a reforming religious element, further emphasizing the medieval barbarization of religion and culture. Protestant writers joined in this condemnation of the dark medieval period, an attack little circumscribed by the defense of the medieval Church by Catholic apologists.

The system of classical education and the standards of classical art employed in the subsequent centuries meant a continuation of the concept established by the humanists. Indeed, the historical philosophy current in the Age of Reason, for purposes of its own, supported the earlier view. Rationalists like Voltaire, Condorcet, Boling-broke, and Hume saw nothing but barbarism, ignorance, superstition, violence, irrationality, and priestly tyranny in the period of Western history between the fall of Rome and the beginning of the modern era, the Renaissance. They also gave currency to the concept of the Italian Renaissance as a period of brilliant culture and irreligion.

It was only in the late eighteenth and early nineteenth century, with the development of the intellectual revolution known as Romanticism, that a reaction took place. A new spirit led the Romanticists to see much in the past to understand and admire. There was a lively interest in historical growth and evolution, including that which took place in the Middle Ages. Human history was enthusiastically approached, the folk origins of art, language, literature, and music were patriotically idealized, and the irrational, the simple, and the emotional sympathetically sought out. The Age of Faith was discovered and peopled with chivalrous knights, beautiful ladies, pious clergy, and industrious peasants. The unity of medieval Christianity and the corporatism of medieval society was admired. Rescuing the Middle Ages from the oblivion to which the classicists and rationalists had relegated it, the Romantic writers found the Renaissance pagan, sensuous, villainous, and shocking — yet attractive.

The astonishing growth of historical research in the nineteenth century produced a great number of works influenced by such varying movements as nationalism, liberalism, Romanticism, neo-classicism, and Hegelian philosophy. The spirit expressed in the art and humanism of the Renaissance received especial consideration. A tendency toward periodization is also characteristic. In the seventh volume (1855) of his *History of France* (1833–62), Jules Michelet, the liberal historian, examined the Renaissance of the sixteenth century in his own country. He saw in medieval civilization the destruction of freedom and the debasement of the human spirit while in the Renaissance came "the discovery of the world and the discovery of man" and the spontaneous rebirth of art and antiquity. Michelet applied the term "Renaissance" to the entire heroic period and not just to art and the classical revival as had been customary. His Renaissance was a distinct epoch, sharply contrasting in spirit with the preceding age.

Five years after Michelet's analysis Jacob Burckhardt formulated the modern traditional interpretation of the Italian Renaissance. Burckhardt's claim to fame is not due to the originality of his ideas and terms, for most of these had been current for centuries. Rather, the greatness of this Swiss historian lay in his ability to make use of the best elements at hand in producing a coherent masterpiece of synthesis in his *Civilization of the Renaissance in Italy* (1860). In his essay, drawn with the masterful hand of a literary artist, Burckhardt sought to lay bare the modern and inner spirit of the Italian Renaissance, approaching the period in a series of topical discussions centering around the civilization as a whole.

Burckhardt's concept of the Italian Renaissance was widely accepted. However, the intellectual, social, and economic phases, which he had neglected, received considerable attention, alteration, or expansion by historians. Renaissance art, also not a part of Burckhardt's essay, was now examined as a product of the spirit and culture of the age. Non-Italian writers related the Renaissance within their own nation to that described by Burckhardt.

While many of the writers of the late nineteenth and early twentieth centuries echo the decisive Burckhardtian synthesis, others began to feel that his harmonious picture of the Italian Renaissance was just too perfect and static. As specialized studies contributed greatly to the knowledge of

other periods, especially that of the Middle Ages, questions began to arise in the minds of historians. Was the contrast between the Renaissance and the medieval period so great? What really brought on the Renaissance in Italy? Were the elements of individualism and modernity unknown before the Renaissance? Was the picture Burckhardt presented true in its delimitations, simplicity, harmony, and construction? Was the Renaissance as pagan and irreligious as depicted? Can science be used as a criterion for the modernity of the Renaissance? A variety of viewpoints on these and other questions are given in the selections which follow.

The marked growth of medieval studies in the twentieth century has been mostly responsible for attacks on Burckhardt's outline and for the creation of the "Problem of the Renaissance." The selected readings which follow present a representative sample of the conflict of opinion on several of the most important aspects of this broad and complex problem.

The two selections following the one from Burckhardt are concerned with its political aspects. The first one, an article by the leading authority on medieval political theory, C. H. McIlwain, stresses the medieval elements in our modern political heritage. He feels that the medieval period was not "one long, dreary epoch of stagnation, of insecurity, of lawless violence." Rather the Middle Ages saw the rise of the very important modern concepts of constitutionalism and the limitation of public authority by private right. In the next excerpt, however, the prominent Renaissance scholar, Hans Baron, reaffirms the Burckhardtian view that the rise of modern political ideas and institutions was one of the distinguishing marks of the Italian Renaissance. He emphasizes the role of the structure and activities of the Italian city-state in producing modern political theory and the pattern of modern government.

In his essay Burckhardt did not give much attention to economic factors or to their effect on the civilization of the Italian Renaissance. In the twentieth century, the relatively new methodologies of psychology, sociology, and economics opened up new approaches for an examination of the civilization of the Renaissance. Prominent among those who used the new methods was Alfred von Martin. Much influenced by the socio-economic writings of Mannheim, Weber, and other German scholars, he sought to analyze the civilization of the Renaissance, "laying bare its roots." Von Martin accepted as essential Burckhardt's periodization, the stress on individualism, and the significance of the Italian Renaissance as the period of transition from the medieval to the modern world. The excerpt from his book, *The Sociology of the Renaissance,* included on page 39, makes evident his conviction that there was a causal relationship between what he describes as "the new dynamic" of capitalism and the characteristics of the Renaissance which Burckhardt had delineated.

While von Martin and others saw the flowering of the Italian Renaissance as the result of vast socio-economic changes, further research and specialized studies in the economic conditions of the Middle Ages and the Renaissance led to qualifications about the brilliant results of economic changes and to some questions about the economic conditions themselves. In the selection by R. S. Lopez which follows Von Martin's the prevailing view of the Italian Renaissance as a brilliant period of dynamic economic expansion is criticized. Professor Lopez feels that the Renaissance in Italy was founded on an earlier medieval economic expansion. In fact, the period of the Renaissance was marked by economic depression, stagnation of population, and excessive taxation. In order to suggest the continuing conflict of opinion on the economic conditions and background of the Renaissance, there has been included in this section dealing with the economic side of the Renaissance problem, an exchange of letters between Lopez and Baron which was originally published in the July, 1956, issue of the *American Historical Review.* They point out the need for more research by economic historians and also the diffi-

culties involved in formulating generalizations about such a complex period as the Renaissance.

Burckhardt had not included very much on science in his outline, but the emphasis which the twentieth century places on the importance of science as one of the most distinctive elements of modern civilization has led later scholars to attempt to evaluate the originality of the Renaissance in this field. In the Renaissance session of the American Historical Association meeting in December, 1941, Professor Dana B. Durand of Mount Holyoke College presented a paper entitled "Tradition and Innovation in Fifteenth-Century Italy." Because of the length and technical complexity of Professor Durand's paper it is not included in the selections which follow, but basing his argument on the lack of evidence of advance in certain technical fields such as map-making and astronomy, he concluded that as far as science and scientific thought are concerned, "the balance of tradition and innovation in fifteenth-century Italy was not so decisively favorable as to distinguish that century radically from those that preceded it, nor to constitute the Quattrocento a unique and unrivaled moment in the history of Western thought."[1] In this same session, however, Dr. Baron presented a paper entitled "Toward a More Positive Evaluation of the Fifteenth-Century Renaissance" which follows as the seventh selection. After a discussion of certain political aspects of the problem (given in an earlier selection of this collection), Dr. Baron turned to the scientific contributions of the Quattrocento. He pointed out that the Burckhardtian thesis of a "Fundamental change in man's outlook on life and the world" included the new scientific approach which has since marked modern civilization.

Professor P. O. Kristeller in remarks also made at this same session examined in some detail the contributions of the humanists to the development of science. He assigned to the Italian humanists an important, if indirect, part in the development of scientific thought, in that they recovered, edited and made more available the body of ancient scientific literature and learning. These remarks, as later published along with the other papers given at this session in the *Journal of the History of Ideas,* appear here as the eighth selection. Another participant, Professor Lynn Thorndike, in contrast to both Baron and Kristeller set forth with great vigor his antipathy toward the whole concept of the "so-called Renaissance." He stressed the unbroken continuity of medieval forms and interests and attacked the originality of the Renaissance in science as well as in other fields. His contribution concludes the group of selections dealing with the problem of science in the Renaissance.

Medieval historians have always been in the forefront of the attack on the Burckhardtian conception of the Renaissance and in the next group of excerpts three prominent medieval scholars present a variety of arguments and evidence in support of this assault.

In his review of "Modern Theories of the Renaissance," Douglas Bush, a professor of literature, evidences a wide-ranging knowledge and keen understanding of the problem of the Renaissance and concludes by placing himself among those who consider that period to be essentially an extension of the Middle Ages. Also in direct opposition to Burckhardt he feels that Italian humanism was strongly Christian in character and not irreligious and pagan.

An even stronger plea for the originality and the primacy of the medieval contribution to modern culture is to be found in the next selection in this group, taken from one of the best known works of the man who was for many years the dean of American medieval historians, Charles Homer Haskins. In this excerpt Professor Haskins points out that many of the elements usually thought of as distinguishing the culture of the Renaissance, such as the revival of the Latin classics, Latin literature, and Greek science and philosophy, are to be found in the twelfth century. In the concluding piece in this group another medi-

[1] *Journal of the History of Ideas,* IV (1943), p. 20.

evalist, the famous Dutch scholar, Johan Huizinga, while ready to accept the term "Renaissance" as a convenient chronological designation, nevertheless sees the period of the fourteenth and fifteenth centuries as terminating the Middle Ages. His views are presented here in an extract from his celebrated study of the cultural history of France and the Netherlands during these two centuries.

Considering the fact that Burckhardt's interpretation of the Renaissance has been challenged by scholars at so many different points, it may seem strange that no one has attempted a new synthetic interpretation of the period. With the appearance of so many specialized studies of various aspects of both the Renaissance and the Middle Ages in the nearly one hundred years since the publication of Burckhardt's essay, it might seem that the groundwork for a new synthesis has been laid. In the next to last selection in this collection, Wallace K. Ferguson draws on his vast knowledge of the literature on the Renaissance to suggest a possible basis for such a work. However, as this collection of readings indicates, Burckhardt has always been supported by able defenders. In the final brief excerpt in this collection, Hans Baron presents his views on the problem of a new synthesis. Taken from a paper delivered by Baron at a session of the convention of the American Historical Association in 1956 which was devoted to a review of Baron's contributions to the study of the Renaissance, it shows sympathy for Ferguson's appeal for a new synthesis but ends by reaffirming Baron's belief in the validity of Burckhardt's thesis that Renaissance Italy was the prototype of the modern world.

Any student who examines the period of the Renaissance is confronted with the necessity of formulating his own answer to the vexing "Problem of the Renaissance." The study of the following selections should assist in this respect. It should also bring the student to the realization of the necessary caution which must be exercised in approaching the interpretations of any historical era or civilization.

The Conflict of Opinion

"We must insist upon it as one of the chief propositions of this book, that it was not the revival of antiquity alone, but its union with the genius of the Italian people, which achieved the conquest of the Western World. . . .

In the character of these states, whether republics or despotism, lies, not the only, but the chief reason for the early development of the Italian. To this it is due that he was the first-born among the sons of Modern Europe. . . .

Since, again, the Italians were the first modern people of Europe who gave themselves boldly to speculation on freedom and necessity, and since they did so under violent and lawless political circumstances, in which evil seemed often to win a splendid and lasting victory, their belief in God began to waver, and their view of the government of the world became fatalistic."

— Jacob Burckhardt

1. Did Renaissance Italy produce the first modern political state?

"In the field of political institutions and ideas I venture to think that what Professor Haskins has termed the Renaissance of the twelfth century marks a more fundamental change than the later developments to which we usually attach the word 'Renaissance'; that the constitutionalism of the modern world owes as much, if not even more, to the twelfth and thirteenth centuries than to any later period of comparable length before the seventeenth." — C. H. McIlwain

"It is because of this survival of civic initiative in geographic proximity to bureaucratic-unifying absolutism that the whole range of modern political experience was traversed in the fifteenth century, and this so rapidly that by the end of the century many of the basic tenets of modern political science had matured, and had been set forth in works of European scope by Machiavelli and Guicciardini."

— Hans Baron

2. Is there an economic basis for the Renaissance in Italy?

"The centre of gravity of medieval society was the land, was the soil. With the Renaissance the economic and thus the social emphasis moves into the town; from the conservative to the liberal, for the town is a changeable and changing element. . . . What was fundamentally new was the rational management of money and the investment of capital. Capital had a creative effect and put a premium on ingenuity and enterprise." — Alfred von Martin

". . . we have to take stock of the now prevalent theory that the Renaissance witnessed a deep economic crisis though not a total catastrophe (are there any total catastrophes in history?), and that in spite of many local, partial, or temporary gains it represented an anticlimax or at least a phase of slower development after the quicker progress of the medieval commercial revolution." — R. S. Lopez

xi

3. Did the Italian Renaissance make original contributions to science?

". . . the balance of tradition and innovation in fifteenth-century Italy was not so decisively favorable as to distinguish that century radically from those that preceded it, not to constitute the Quattrocento a unique and unrivaled moment in the history of western thought."

— DANA B. DURAND

"The influence of humanism on science as well as on philosophy was indirect, but powerful. The actual performance of the humanists in these fields was rather poor. But they popularized the entire body of ancient Greek learning and literature and thus made available new source materials of which the professional scientists and philosophers could not fail to take advantage."

— PAUL O. KRISTELLER

"Not only has it been demonstrated that the thirteenth and fourteenth centuries were more active and penetrating in natural science than was the Quattrocento, but the notion that 'appreciation of natural beauty' was 'introduced into modern Europe by the Italian Renaissance' must also be abandoned."

— LYNN THORNDIKE

4. Can we still retain the periodic concept of the Renaissance?

"The Middle Ages exhibit life and color and change, much eager search after knowledge and beauty, much creative accomplishment in art, in literature, in institutions. The Italian Renaissance was preceded by similar, if less wide-reaching movements; indeed it came out of the Middle Ages so gradually that historians are not agreed when it began, and some would go so far as to abolish the name, and perhaps even the fact, of a renaissance in the Quattrocento."

— CHARLES HOMER HASKINS

"Viewing the Renaissance as an age in the history of Western Europe, then, I would define it as the age of transition from medieval to modern civilization, a period characterized primarily by the gradual shift from one fairly well co-ordinated and clearly defined type of civilization to another, yet, at the same time, possessing in its own right certain distinctive traits and a high degree of cultural vitality. And on the basis of this concept or hypothesis, I would set the arbitrary dates — 1300 to 1600 — as its chronological boundaries."

— WALLACE K. FERGUSON

"Today, a hundred years after Burckhardt — so I would argue — culture, as well as opinions as to the value of Humanism for our world, have so profoundly changed that for the first time the limitations of the Burckhardtian pattern of reference can be fully grasped, although his fundamental discovery, that Renaissance Italy somehow was a prototype of the modern world, has preserved its truth."

— HANS BARON

THE CIVILIZATION OF THE RENAISSANCE IN ITALY

JACOB BURCKHARDT

THE STATE AS A WORK OF ART

Introduction

This work bears the title of an essay in the strictest sense of the word. No one is more conscious than the writer with what limited means and strength he has addressed himself to a task so arduous. And even if he could look with greater confidence upon his own researches he would hardly thereby feel more assured of the approval of competent judges. To each eye, perhaps, the outlines of a given civilization present a different picture; and in treating of a civilization which is the mother of our own, and whose influence is still at work among us, it is unavoidable that individual judgment and feeling should tell every moment both on the writer and on the reader. In the wide ocean upon which we venture, the possible ways and directions are many; and the same studies which have served for this work might easily, in other hands, not only receive a wholly different treatment and application, but lead also to essentially different conclusions. Such indeed is the importance of the subject, that it calls for fresh investigation, and may be studied with advantage from the most varied points of view. Meanwhile we are content if a patient hearing is granted us, and if this book be taken and judged as a whole. It is the most serious difficulty of the history of civilization that a great intellectual process must be broken up into single, and often into what seem arbitrary categories, in order to be in any way intelligible. It was formerly our intention to fill up the gaps in this book by a special work on the "Art of the Renaissance" — an intention, however, which we have been able only to fulfill in part. The struggle between the Popes and the Hohenstaufen left Italy in a political condition which differed essentially from that of other countries of the West. While in France, Spain, and England the feudal system was so organized that, at the close of its existence, it was naturally transformed into a unified monarchy, and while in Germany it helped to maintain, at least outwardly, the unity of the empire, Italy had shaken it off almost entirely. The Emperors of the fourteenth century, even in the most favorable case, were no longer received and respected as feudal lords, but as possible leaders and supporters of powers already in existence; while the Papacy, with its creatures and allies, was strong enough to hinder national unity in the future, not strong enough itself to bring about that unity. Between the two lay a multitude of political units — republics and despots — in part of long standing, in part of recent origin, whose existence was founded simply on their power to maintain it. In them for the first time we detect the modern political spirit of Europe, surrendered freely to its own instincts, often displaying the worst features of an unbridled egotism, outraging every right, and killing every germ of a

From Jacob Burckhardt, *The Civilization of the Period of the Renaissance in Italy*, Trans. by S. G. C. Middlemore (London, 1878), Vol. I, pp. 3–17, 85–86, 103–120, 181–190, 191–197, 239–242, 245–246, 283–285; Vol. II, pp. 3–20, 35–37, 42–43, 46, 109–116, 246–247, 297–301, 305, 309–317, 318–320.

healthier culture. But, wherever this vicious tendency is overcome or in any way compensated, a new fact appears in history — the state as the outcome of reflection and calculation, the state as a work of art. This new life displays itself in a hundred forms, both in the republican and in the despotic states, and determines their inward constitution, no less than their foreign policy. We shall limit ourselves to the consideration of the completer and more clearly defined type, which is offered by the despotic states.

The internal condition of the despotically governed states had a memorable counterpart in the Norman Empire of Lower Italy and Sicily, after its transformation by the Emperor Frederick II. Bred amid treason and peril in the neighborhood of the Saracens, Frederick, the first ruler of the modern type who sat upon a throne, had early accustomed himself, both in criticism and action, to a thoroughly objective treatment of affairs. His acquaintance with the internal condition and administration of the Saracenic states was close and intimate; and the mortal struggle in which he was engaged with the Papacy compelled him, no less than his adversaries, to bring into the field all the resources at his command. Frederick's measures (especially after the year 1231) are aimed at the complete destruction of the feudal state, at the transformation of the people into a multitude destitute of will and of the means of resistance, but profitable in the utmost degree to the exchequer. He centralized, in a manner hitherto unknown in the West, the whole judicial and political administration by establishing the right of appeal from the feudal courts, which he did not, however, abolish, to the imperial judges. No office was henceforth to be filled by popular election, under penalty of the devastation of the offending district and of the enslavement of its inhabitants. Excise duties were introduced; the taxes, based on a comprehensive assessment, and distributed in accordance with Mohammedan usages, were collected by those cruel and vexatious methods without which, it is true, it is impossible to obtain any money from Orientals. Here, in short, we find, not a people, but simply a disciplined multitude of subjects; who were forbidden, for example, to marry out of the country without special permission, and under no circumstances were allowed to study abroad. The University of Naples was the first we know of to restrict the freedom of study, while the East, in these respects at all events, left its youth unfettered. It was after the example of Mohammedan rulers that Frederick traded on his own account in all parts of the Mediterranean, reserving to himself the monopoly of many commodities, and restricting in various ways the commerce of his subjects. The Fatimite Caliphs, with all their esoteric unbelief, were, at least in their earlier history, tolerant of all the differences in the religious faith of their people; Frederick, on the other hand, crowned his system of government by a religious inquisition, which will seem the more reprehensible when we remember that in the persons of the heretics he was persecuting the representatives of a free municipal life. Lastly, the internal police, and the kernel of the army for foreign service, was composed of Saracens who had been brought over from Sicily to Nocera and Luceria — men who were deaf to the cry of misery and careless of the ban of the Church. At a later period the subjects, by whom the use of weapons had long been forgotten, were passive witnesses of the fall of Manfred and of the seizure of the government by Charles of Anjou; the latter continued to use the system which he found already at work.

At the side of the centralizing Emperor appeared an usurper of the most peculiar kind: his vicar and son-in-law, Ezzelino de Romano. He stands as the representative of no system of government or administration, for all his activity was wasted in struggles for supremacy in the eastern part of Upper Italy; but as a political type he was a figure of no less importance for the future than his imperial protector Frederick. The conquests and usurpations which had hitherto taken place in the Middle Ages rested on real or pretended inheritance and other such claims, or else were effected against unbelievers and excommunicated persons. Here for the first time the attempt was openly made to found a throne by wholesale murder and endless barbarities, by the adoption, in short, of any means with a view to nothing but the end pursued. None of his successors, not even Cesar Borgia, rivalled the colossal guilt of Ezzelino; but the example once set was not forgotten, and his fall led to no return of justice among the nations, and served as no warning to future transgressors.

It was in vain at such a time that St. Thomas Aquinas, a born subject of Frederick, set up the theory of a constitutional monarchy, in which the prince was to be supported by an upper house named by himself, and a representative body elected by the people; in vain did he concede to the people the right of revolution. Such theories found no echo outside the lecture-room, and Frederick and Ezzelino were and remain for Italy the great political phenomena of the thirteenth century. Their personality, already half legendary, forms the most important subject of "The Hundred Old Tales" whose original composition falls certainly within this century. In them Frederick is already represented as possessing the right to do as he pleased with the property of his subjects, and exercises on all, even on criminals, a profound influence by the force of his personality; Ezzelino is spoken of with the awe which all mighty impressions leave behind them. His person became the centre of a whole literature, from the chronicle of eye-witnesses to the half-mythical tragedy of later poets.

The Tyranny of the Fourteenth Century

The tyrannies, great and small, of the fourteenth century afford constant proof that examples such as these were not thrown away. Their crimes, which were fearful, have been fully told by historians. As states depending for existence on themselves alone, and scientifically organized with a view to this object, they present to us a higher interest than that of mere narrative.

The deliberate adaptation of means to ends, of which no prince out of Italy had at that time a conception, joined to almost absolute power within the limits of the state, produced among the despots both men and modes of life of a peculiar character. The chief secret of government in the hands of the prudent ruler lay in leaving the incidence of taxation so far as possible where he found it, or as he had first arranged it. The chief sources of income were: a land tax, based on a valuation; definite taxes on articles of consumption and duties on exported and imported goods; together with the private fortune of the ruling house. The only possible increase was derived from the growth of business and of general prosperity. Loans, such as we find in the free cities, were here unknown; a well-planned confiscation was held a preferable means of raising money, provided only that it left public credit unshaken — an end attained, for example, by the truly Oriental practice of deposing and plundering the director of the finances.

Out of this income the expenses of the little court, of the body-guard, of the mercenary troops, and of the public buildings were met, as well as of the buffoons and men of talent who belonged to the personal attendants of the prince. The illegitimacy of his rule isolated the tyrant and surrounded him with constant danger; the most honorable alliance which he could form was with intellectual merit, without regard to its origin. The liberality of the northern princes of the thirteenth century was confined to the knights, to the nobility which served and sang. It was otherwise with the Italian despot. With his thirst for fame and his passion for monumental works, it was talent, not birth, which he needed. In the company of the poet and the scholar he felt himself in a new position, almost, indeed, in possession of a new legitimacy.

No prince was more famous in this respect than the ruler of Verona, Can Grande della Scala, who numbered among the illustrious exiles whom he entertained at his court representatives of the whole of Italy. The men of letters were not ungrateful. Petrarch, whose visits at the courts of such men have been so severely censured, sketched an ideal picture of a prince of the fourteenth century. He demands great things from his patron, the lord of Padua, but in a manner which shows that he holds him capable of them. "Thou must not be the master but the father of thy subjects, and must love them as thy children; yea, as members of thy body. Weapons, guards, and soldiers thou mayest employ against the enemy — with thy subjects goodwill is sufficient. By citizens, of course, I mean those who love the existing order; for those who daily desire change are rebels and traitors, and against such a stern justice may take its course."

Here follows, worked out in detail, the purely modern fiction of the omnipotence of the State. The prince is to be independent of his courtiers, but at the same time to govern with simplicity and modesty; he is to take everything into his charge, to maintain and restore churches and public buildings, to keep up the municipal police, to drain the marshes, to look after the supply of wine and corn; he is to exercise a strict justice, so to distribute the taxes that the people can recognize their necessity and the regret of the ruler to put his hands into the pockets of others; he is to support the sick and the helpless, and to give his protection and society to distinguished scholars, on whom his fame in after ages will depend.

But whatever might be the brighter sides of the system, and the merits of individual rulers, yet the men of the fourteenth century were not without a more or less distinct consciousness of the brief and uncertain tenure of most of these despotisms. Inasmuch as political institutions like these are naturally secure in proportion to the size of the territory in which they exist, the larger principalities were constantly tempted to swallow up the smaller. Whole heca-

tombs of petty rulers were sacrificed at this time to the Visconti alone. As a result of this outward danger an inward ferment was in ceaseless activity; and the effect of the situation on the character of the ruler was generally of the most sinister kind. Absolute power, with its temptations to luxury and unbridled selfishness, and the perils to which he was exposed from enemies and conspirators, turned him almost inevitably into a tyrant in the worst sense of the word. Well for him if he could trust his nearest relations! But where all was illegitimate, there could be no regular law of inheritance, either with regard to the succession or to the division of the ruler's property; and consequently the heir, if incompetent or a minor, was liable in the interest of the family itself to be supplanted by an uncle or cousin of more resolute character. The acknowledgement or exclusion of the bastards was a fruitful source of contest; and most of these families in consequence were plagued with a crowd of discontented and vindictive kinsmen. This circumstance gave rise to continual outbreaks of treason and to frightful scenes of domestic bloodshed. Sometimes the pretenders lived abroad in exile, and like the Visconti, who practised the fisherman's craft on the Lake of Garda, viewed the situation with patient indifference. When asked by a messenger of his rival when and how he thought of returning to Milan, he gave the reply, "By the same means as those by which I was expelled, but not till his crimes have outweighed my own." Sometimes, too, the despot was sacrificed by his relations, with the view of saving the family, to the public conscience which he had too grossly outraged. In a few cases the government was in the hands of the whole family, or at least the ruler was bound to take their advice; and here, too, the distribution of property and influence led to bitter disputes.

The whole of this system excited the deep and persistent hatred of the Florentine writers of that epoch. Even the pomp and display with which the despot was perhaps less anxious to gratify his own vanity than to impress the popular imagination, awakened their keenest sarcasm. Woe to an adventurer if he fell into their hands, like the upstart Doge Aguello of Pisa (1364), who used to ride out with a golden sceptre, and show himself at the window of his house, "as relics are shown," reclining on embroidered drapery and cushions, served like a pope or emperor, by kneeling attendants. More often, however, the old Florentines speak on this subject in a tone of lofty seriousness. Dante saw and characterized well the vulgarity and commonplace which mark the ambition of the new princes. "What mean their trumpets and their bells, their horns and their flutes; but come, hangman — come, vultures?" The castle of the tyrant, as pictured by the popular mind, is a lofty and solitary building, full of dungeons and listening-tubes, the home of cruelty and misery. Misfortune is foretold to all who enter the service of the despot, who even becomes at last himself an object of pity: he must needs be the enemy of all good and honest men; he can trust no one, and can read in the faces of his subjects the expectation of his fall. "As despotisms rise, grow, and are consolidated, so grows in their midst the hidden element which must produce their dissolution and ruin." But the deepest ground of dislike has not been stated; Florence was then the scene of the richest development of human individuality, while for the despots no other individuality could be suffered to live and thrive but their own and that of their nearest dependents. The control of the individual was rigorously carried out, even down to the establishment of a system of passports.

The astrological superstitions and the religious unbelief of many of the tyrants gave, in the minds of their contemporaries, a peculiar color to this awful and Godforsaken existence. When the last Carrara could no longer defend the walls and gates of the plague-stricken Padua, hemmed in on all sides by the Venetians (1405), the soldiers of the guard heard him cry to the devil "to come and kill him.". . .

The Republics: Venice and Florence

The Italian municipalities had, in earlier days, given signal proof of that force which transforms the city into the state. It remained only that these cities should combine in a great confederation; and this idea was constantly recurring to Italian statesmen, whatever differences of form it might from time to time display. In fact, during the struggles of the twelfth and thirteenth centuries, great and formidable leagues actually were formed by the cities; and Sismondi is of opinion that the time of the final armaments of the Lombard confederation against Barbarossa [from 1168 on] was the moment when a universal Italian league was possible. But the more powerful states had already developed characteristic features which made any such scheme impracticable. In their commercial dealings they shrank from no measures, however extreme, which might damage their competitors; they held their weaker neighbours in a condition of helpless dependence — in short, they each fancied they could get on by themselves without the assistance of the rest, and thus paved the way for future usurpation. The usurper was forthcoming when long conflicts between the nobility and the people, and between the different factions of the nobility, had awakened the desire for a strong government, and when bands of mercenaries ready and willing to sell their aid to the highest bidder had superseded the general levy of the citizens which party leaders now found unsuited to their purposes. The tyrants destroyed the freedom of most of the cities; here and there they were expelled, but not thoroughly, or only for a short time; and they were always restored, since the inward conditions were favorable to them, and the opposing forces were exhausted.

Among the cities which maintained their independence are two of deep significance for the history of the human race: Florence, the city of incessant movement, which has left us a record of the thoughts and aspirants of each and all who, for three centuries, took part in this movement, and

Venice, the city of apparent stagnation and political secrecy. No contrast can be imagined stronger than that which is offered us by these two, and neither can be compared to anything else which the world has hitherto produced. . . .

The most elevated political thought and the most varied forms of human development are found united in the history of Florence, which in this sense deserves the name of the first modern state in the world. Here the whole people are busied with what in the despotic cities is the affair of a single family. That wondrous Florentine spirit, at once keenly critical and artistically creative, was incessantly transforming the social and political condition of the state, and as incessantly describing and judging the change. Florence thus became the home of political doctrines and theories, of experiments and sudden changes, but also, like Venice, the home of statistical science, and alone and above all other states in the world, the home of historical representation in the modern sense of the phrase. The spectacle of ancient Rome and a familiarity with its leading writers were not without influence; Giovanni Villani confesses that he received the first impulse to his great work at the jubilee of the year 1300, and began it immediately on his return home. Yet how many among the 200,000 pilgrims of that year may have been like him in gifts and tendencies, and still did not write the history of their native cities! For not all of them could encourage themselves with the thought: "Rome is sinking; my native city is rising, and ready to achieve great things and therefore I wish to relate its past history, and hope to continue the story of the present time, and as long as my life shall last." And besides the witness to its past, Florence obtained through its historians something further — a greater fame than fell to the lot of any other city of Italy.

Our present task is not to write the history of this remarkable state, but merely to give a few indications of the intellectual freedom and independence for which the Florentines were indebted to this history.

In no other city of Italy were the struggles of political parties so bitter, of such early origin, and so permanent. The descriptions of them, which belong, it is true, to a somewhat later period, give clear evidence of the superiority of Florentine criticism.

And what a politician is the great victim of these crises, Dante Alighieri, matured alike by home and by exile! He uttered his scorn of the incessant changes and experiments in the constitution of his native city in verses of adamant, which will remain proverbial so long as political events of the same kind recur; he addressed his home in words of defiance and yearning which must have stirred the hearts of his countrymen. But his thoughts ranged over Italy and the whole world; and if his passion for the Empire, as he conceived it, was no more than an illusion, it must yet be admitted that the youthful dreams of a new-born political speculation are in his case not without a poetical grandeur. He is proud to be the first who trod this path, certainly in the footsteps of Aristotle, but in his own way independently. His ideal emperor is a just and humane judge, dependent on God only, the heir of the universal sway of Rome to which belonged the sanction of nature, of right and of the will of God. The conquest of the world was, according to this view, rightful, resting on a divine judgment between Rome and the other nations of the earth, and God gave his approval to this empire, since under it he became Man, submitting at his birth to the census of the Emperor Augustus, and at his death to the judgment of Pontius Pilate. We may find it hard to appreciate these and other arguments of the same kind, but Dante's passion never fails to carry us with him. In his letters he appears as one of the earliest publicists, and is perhaps the first layman to publish political tracts in this form. He began early. Soon after the death of Beatrice he addressed a pamphlet on the state of Florence "to the Great ones of the Earth," and the public utterances of his later years, dating from the time of his banishment, are all directed to emperors, princes, and cardinals. In these letters and in his book "De Vulgari Eloquio" the feeling, bought with such bitter pains, is constantly recurring that the exile may find elsewhere than in his native place an intellectual home in language and culture, which cannot be taken from him. On this point we shall have more to say in the sequel.

To the two Villani, Giovanni as well as Matteo, we owe not so much deep political reflexion as fresh and practical observations, together with the elements of Florentine statistics and important notices of other states. Here too trade and commerce had given the impulse to economical as well as political science. Nowhere else in the world was such accurate information to be had on financial affairs. The wealth of the Papal court at Avignon, which at the death of John XXII amounted to twenty-five millions of gold florins, would be incredible on any less trustworthy authority. Here only, at Florence, do we meet with colossal loans like that which the King of England contracted from the Florentine houses of Bardi and Peruzzi, who lost to his Majesty the sum of 1,365,000 gold florins (1338) — their own money and that of their partners — and nevertheless recovered from the shock. Most important facts are here recorded as to the condition of Florence at this time; the public income (over 300,000 gold florins) and expenditure; the population of the city, here only roughly estimated, according to the consumption of bread, in "bocche," i.e. mouths, put at 90,000, and the population of the whole territory; the excess of 300 to 500 male children among the 5,800 to 6,000 annually baptised; the school-children, of whom 8,000 to 10,000 learned reading, 1,000 to 1,200 in six schools arithmetic; and besides these, 600 scholars who were taught Latin grammar and logic in four schools. Then follow the statistics of the churches and monasteries; of the hospitals, which held more than a thousand beds; of the wooltrade, with most valuable details; of the

mint, the provisioning of the city, the public officials, and so on. Incidentally we learn many curious facts; how, for instance, when the public funds ("monte") were first established, in the year 1353, the Franciscans spoke from the pulpit in favour of the measure, the Dominicans and Augustinians against it. The economical results of the black death were and could be observed and described nowhere else in all Europe as in this city. Only a Florentine could have left it on record how it was expected that the scanty population would have made everything cheap, and how instead of that labor and commodities doubled in price; how the common people at first would do no work at all, but simply give themselves up to enjoyment; how in the city itself servants and maids were not to be had except at extravagant wages; how the peasants would only till the best lands, and left the rest uncultivated; and how the enormous legacies bequeathed to the poor at the time of the plague seemed afterwards useless, since the poor had either died or had ceased to be poor. Lastly, on the occasion of a great bequest, by which a childless philanthropist left six "danari" to every beggar in the city, the attempt is made to give a comprehensive statistical account of Florentine mendicancy.

This statistical view of things was at a later time still more highly cultivated at Florence. The noteworthy point about it is that, as a rule, we can perceive its connection with the higher aspects of history, with art, and with culture in general. An inventory of the year 1422 mentions, within the compass of the same document, the seventy-two exchange offices which surrounded the "Mercato Nuovo"; the amount of coined money in circulation (two million golden florins); the then new industry of gold spinning; the silk wares, Filippo Brunellesco, then busy in digging classical architecture from its grave; and Lionardo Aretino, secretary of the republic, at work at the revival of ancient literature and eloquence; lastly, it speaks of the general prosperity of the city, then free from political conflicts, and of the good fortune of Italy, which had rid itself of foreign mercenaries. The Venetian statistics quoted above which date from about the same year, certainly give evidence of larger property and profits and of a more extensive scene of action; Venice had long been mistress of the seas before Florence sent out its first galleys (1422) to Alexandria. But no reader can fail to recognize the higher spirit of the Florentine documents. These and similar lists recur at intervals of ten years, systematically arranged and tabulated, while elsewhere we find at best occasional notices. We can form an approximate estimate of the property and the business of the first Medici; they paid for charities, public buildings, and taxes from 1434 to 1471 no less than 663,755 gold florins, of which more than 400,000 fell on Cosimo alone, and Lorenzo Magnifico was delighted that the money had been so well spent. In 1472 we have again a most important and in its way complete view of the commerce and trades of this city, some of which may be wholly or partly reckoned among the fine arts — such as those which had to do with damasks and gold or silver embroidery, with wood-carving and "intarsia," with the sculpture of arabesques in marble and sandstone, with portraits in wax, and with jewellery and work in gold. The inborn talent of the Florentines for the systematization of outward life is shown by their books on agriculture, business, and domestic economy, which are markedly superior to those of other European people in the fifteenth century. It has been rightly decided to publish selections of these works, although no little study will be needed to extract clear and definite results from them. At all events, we have no difficulty in recognizing the city, where dying parents begged the government in their wills to fine their sons 1,000 florins if they declined to practise a regular profession.

For the first half of the sixteenth century probably no state in the world possesses a document like the magnificent description of Florence by Varchi. In descriptive statis-tics, as in so many things besides, yet another model is left to us, before the freedom and greatness of the city sank into the grave.

This statistical estimate of outward life is, however, uniformly accompanied by the narrative of political events to which we have already referred.

Florence not only existed under political forms more varied than those of the free states of Italy and of Europe generally, but it reflected upon them far more deeply. It is a faithful mirror of the relations of individuals and classes to a variable whole. The pictures of the great civic democracies in France and in Flanders, as they are delineated in Froissart, and the narratives of the German chroniclers of the fourteenth century, are in truth of high importance; but in comprehensiveness of thought and in the rational development of the story, none will bear comparison with the Florentines. The rule of the nobility, the tyrannies, the struggles of the middle class with the proletariat, limited and unlimited democracy, pseudo-democracy, the primacy of a single house, the theocracy of Savonarola, and the mixed forms of government which prepared the way for the Medicean despotism — all are so described that the inmost motives of the actors are laid bare to the light. At length Machiavelli in his Florentine history (down to 1492) represents his native city as a living organism and its development as a natural and individual process; he is the first of the moderns who has risen to such a conception. It lies without our province to determine whether and in what points Machiavelli may have done violence to history, as is notoriously the case in his life of Castruccio Castracani — a fancy picture of the typical despot. We might find something to say against every line of the "Istorie Fiorentine," and yet the great and unique value of the whole would remain unaffected. And his contemporaries and successors, Jacopo Pitti, Guicciardini, Segni, Varchi, Vettori, what a circle of illustrious names! And what a story it is which these masters tell us! The great and memorable drama of the last decades of the Florentine republic is here unfolded. The voluminous record of the collapse of the highest and most original life which the world could then show may appear to one but as a collection of curiosities, may awaken in another a devilish delight at the shipwreck of so much nobility and grandeur, to a third may seem like a great historical assize; for all it will be an object of thought and study to the end of time. The evil, which was for ever troubling the peace of the city, was its rule over once powerful and now conquered rivals like Pisa — a rule of which the necessary consequence was a chronic state of violence. The only remedy, certainly an extreme one and which none but Savonarola could have persuaded Florence to accept, and that only with the help of favorable chances, would have been the well-timed resolution of Tuscany into a federal union of free cities. At a later period this scheme, then no more than the dream of a past age, brought (1548) a patriotic citizen of Lucca to the scaffold. From this evil and from the ill-starred Guelph sympathies of Florence for a foreign prince, which familiarized it with foreign intervention, came all the disasters which followed. But who does not admire the people, which was wrought up by its venerated preacher to a mood of such sustained loftiness, that for the first time in Italy it set the example of sparing a conquered foe, while the whole history of its past taught nothing but vengeance and extermination? The glow which melted patriotism into one with moral regeneration may seem, when looked at from a distance, to have soon passed away; but its best results shine forth again in the memorable siege of 1529–30. They were "fools," as Guicciardini then wrote, who drew down this storm upon Florence, but he confesses himself that they achieved things which seemed incredible; and when he declares that sensible people would have got out of the way of the danger, he means no more than that Florence ought to have yielded itself silently and ingloriously into the hands of its enemies. It would no doubt have preserved its splendid suburbs and gardens, and the lives and prosperity of countless citizens; but it would have been the poorer by one of its greatest and most ennobling memories.

In many of their chief merits the Florentines are the pattern and the earliest type of Italians and modern Europeans generally; they are so also in many of their defects. When Dante compares the city which was always mending its constitution with the sick man who is continually changing his posture to escape from pain, he touches with the comparison a permanent feature of the political life of Florence. The great modern fallacy that a constitution can be made, can be manufactured by a combination of existing forces and tendencies, was constantly cropping up in stormy times; even Machiavelli is not wholly free from it. Constitutional artists were never wanting who by an ingenious distribution and division of political power, by indirect elections of the most complicated kind, by the establishment of nominal offices, sought to found a lasting order of things, and to satisfy or to deceive the rich and the poor alike. They naïvely fetch their examples from classical antiquity, and borrow the party names "ottimati," "aristocrazia," as a matter of course. The world since then has become used to these expressions and given them a conventional European sense, whereas all former party names were purely national, and either characterized the cause at issue or sprang from the caprice of accident. But how a name colors or discolors a political cause!

But of all who thought it possible to construct a state, the greatest beyond all comparison was Machiavelli. He treats existing forces as living and active, takes a large and an accurate view of alternative possibilities, and seeks to mislead neither himself nor others. No man could be freer from vanity or ostentation; indeed, he does not write for the public but either for princes and administrators or for personal friends. The danger for him does not lie in an affectation of genius or in a false order of ideas, but rather in a powerful imagination which he evidently controls with difficulty. The objectivity of his political judgment is sometimes appalling in its sincerity; but it is the sign of a time of no ordinary need and peril, when it was a hard matter to believe in right, or to credit others with just dealing. Virtuous indignation at his expense is thrown away upon us who have seen in what sense political morality is understood by the statesmen of our own century. Machiavelli was at all events able to forget himself in his cause. In truth, although his writings, with the exception of very few words, are altogether destitute of enthusiasm, and although the Florentines themselves treated him at last as a criminal, he was a patriot in the fullest meaning of the word. But free as he was, like most of his contemporaries, in speech and morals, the welfare of the state was yet his first and last thought.

His most complete programme for the construction of a new political system at Florence is set forth in the memorial to Leo X, composed after the death of the younger Lorenzo Medici, Duke of Urbino (d. 1519), to whom he had dedicated his "Prince." The State was by that time in extremities and utterly corrupt, and the remedies proposed are not always morally justifiable; but it is most interesting to see how he hopes to set up the republic in the form of a moderate democracy, as heiress to the Medici. A more ingenious scheme of concessions to the Pope, to the Pope's various adherents, and to the different Florentine interests, cannot be imagined; we might fancy ourselves looking into the works of a clock. Principles, observations, comparisons, political forecasts, and the like are to be found in numbers in the "Discorsi," among them flashes of wonderful insight. He recognizes, for example, the law of a continuous though not uniform development in republican institutions, and requires the constitution to be flexible and capable of change, as the only means of dispensing with bloodshed and banishments. For a like reason, in order to guard against private violence and foreign inter-

ference — "the death of all freedom" — he wishes to see introduced a judicial procedure ("accusa") against hated citizens, in place of which Florence had hitherto had nothing but the court of scandal. With a masterly hand the tardy and involuntary decisions are characterized, which at critical moments play so important a part in republican states. Once, it is true, he is misled by his imagination and the pressure of events into unqualified praise of the people, which chooses its officers, he says, better than any prince, and which can be cured of its errors by "good advice." With regard to the Government of Tuscany, he has no doubt that it belongs to his native city, and maintains, in a special "Discorso" that the reconquest of Pisa is a question of life or death; he deplores that Arezzo, after the rebellion of 1502, was not razed to the ground; he admits in general that Italian republics must be allowed to expand freely and add to their territory in order to enjoy peace at home, and not to be themselves attacked by others, but declares that Florence had always begun at the wrong end, and from the first made deadly enemies of Pisa, Lucca, and Siena, while Pistoja, "treated like a brother," had voluntarily submitted to her. . . .

THE DEVELOPMENT OF THE INDIVIDUAL

The Italian State and the Individual

In the character of these states, whether republics or despotisms, lies, not the only, but the chief reason for the early development of the Italian. To this it is due that he was the first-born among the sons of modern Europe.

In the Middle Ages both sides of human consciousness — that which was turned within as that which was turned without — lay dreaming or half-awake beneath a common veil. The veil was woven of faith, illusion, and childish prepossession, through which the world and history were seen clad in strange hues. Man was conscious of himself only as a member of a race, people, party, family, or corporation — only through some general category. In Italy this veil first melted into air; an *objective* treatment and consideration of the State and of all the things of this world became possible. The *subjective* side at the same time asserted itself with corresponding emphasis; man became a spiritual *individual,* and recognized himself as such. In the same way the Greek had once distinguished himself from the barbarian, and the Arabian had felt himself an individual at a time when other Asiatics knew themselves only as members of a race. It will not be difficult to show that this result was owing above all to the political circumstances of Italy.

In far earlier times we can here and there detect a development of free personality which in Northern Europe either did not occur at all, or could not display itself in the same manner. The band of audacious wrongdoers in the sixteenth century described to us by Luidprand, some of the contemporaries of Gregory VII, and a few of the opponents of the first Hohenstaufen, show us characters of this kind, but at the close of the thirteenth century Italy began to swarm with individuality; the charm laid upon human personality was dissolved; and a thousand figures meet us each in its own special shape and dress. Dante's great poem would have been impossible in any other country of Europe, if only for the reason that they all still lay under the spell of race. For Italy the august poet, through the wealth of individuality which he set forth, was the most national herald of his time. But this unfolding of the treasures of human nature in literature and art — this many-sided representation and criticism — will be discussed in separate chapters; here we have to deal only with the psychological fact itself. This fact appears in the most decisive and unmistakable form. The Italians of the fourteenth century knew little of false modesty or of hypocrisy in any shape; not one of them was afraid of singularity, of being and seeming unlike his neighbors.

Despotism, as we have already seen, fostered in the highest degree the individuality not only of the tyrant or Condottiere himself, but also of the men whom he protected or used as his tools — the secretary, minister, poet, and companion. These people were forced to know all the inward resources of their own nature, passing or permanent; and their enjoyment of life was enhanced and concentrated by the desire to obtain the greatest satisfaction from a possibly very brief period of power and influence.

But even the subjects whom they ruled over were not free from the same impulse. Leaving out of account those who wasted their lives in secret opposition and conspiracies, we speak of the majority who were content with a strictly private station, like most of the urban population of the Byzantine empire and the Mohammedan states. No doubt it was often hard for the subjects of a Visconti to maintain the dignity of their persons and families, and multitudes must have lost in moral character through the servitude they lived under. But this was not the case with regard to individuality; for political impotence does not hinder the different tendencies and manifestations of private life from thriving in the fullest vigor and variety. Wealth and culture, so far as display and rivalry were not forbidden to them, a municipal freedom which did not cease to be considerable, and a Church which, unlike that of the Byzantine or of the Mohammedan world, was not identical with the State — all these conditions undoubtedly favored the growth of individual thought, for which the necessary leisure was furnished by the cessation of party conflicts. The private man, indifferent to politics, and busied partly with serious pursuits, partly with the interests of a *dilettante,* seems to have been first fully formed in these despotisms of the fourteenth century. Documentary evidence cannot, of course, be required on such a point. The novelists, from whom we might expect information, describe to us oddities in plenty, but only from one point of view and in so far as the needs of the story demand. Their scene, too, lies chiefly in the republican cities.

In the latter, circumstances were also, but in another way, favorable to the growth of individual character. The more frequently the governing party was changed, the more the individual was led to make the utmost of the exercise and enjoyment of power. The statesmen and popular leaders, especially in Florentine history, acquired so marked a personal character, that we can scarcely find, even exceptionally, a parallel to them in contemporary history, hardly even in Jacob von Arteveldt.

The members of the defeated parties, on the other hand, often came into a position like that of the subjects of the despotic States, with the difference that the freedom or power already enjoyed, and in some cases the hope of recovering them, gave a higher energy to their individuality. Among these men of involuntary leisure we find, for instance, an Agnolo Pandolfini (d. 1446), whose work on domestic economy is the first complete program of a developed private life. His estimate of the duties of the individual as against the dangers and thanklessness of public life is in its way a true monument of the age.

Banishment, too, has this effect above all, that it either wears the exile out or develops whatever is greatest in him. "In all our more populous cities," says Gioviano Pontano, "we see a crowd of people who have left their homes of their own free will; but a man takes his virtues with him wherever he goes." And, in fact, they were by no means only men who had been actually exiled, but thousands left their native place voluntarily, because they found its political or economical condition intolerable. The Florentine emigrants at Ferrara and the Lucchese in Venice formed whole colonies by themselves.

The cosmopolitanism which grew up in the most gifted circles is in itself a high stage of individualism. Dante, as we have already said, finds a new home in the language and culture of Italy, but goes beyond even this in the words, "My country is the whole world." And when his recall to Florence was offered him on unworthy con-ditions, he wrote back: "Can I not everywhere behold the light of the sun and the stars; everywhere meditate on the noblest truths, without appearing ingloriously and shamefully before the city and the people. Even my bread will not fail me." The artists exult no less defiantly in their freedom from the constraints of fixed residence. "Only he who has learned everything," says Ghiberti, "is nowhere a stranger; robbed of his fortune and without friends, he is yet the citizen of every country, and can fearlessly despise the changes of fortune." In the same strain an exiled humanist writes: "Wherever a learned man fixes his seat, there is home."

The Perfecting of the Individual

An acute and practised eye might be able to trace, step by step, the increase in the number of complete men during the fifteenth century. Whether they had before them as a conscious object the harmonious development of their spiritual and material existence, is hard to say; but several of them attained it, so far as is consistent with the imperfection of all that is earthly. It may be better to renounce the attempt at an estimate of the share which fortune, character, and talent had in the life of Lorenzo Magnifico. But look at a personality like that of Ariosto, especially as shown in his satires. In what harmony are there expressed the pride of the man and the poet, the irony with which he treats his own enjoyments, the most delicate satire, and the deepest goodwill!

When this impulse to the highest individual development was combined with a powerful and varied nature, which had mastered all the elements of the culture of the age, then arose the "all-sided man" — "l'uomo universale" — who belonged to Italy alone. Men there were of encyclopaedic knowledge in many countries during the Middle Ages, for this knowledge was confined within narrow limits; and even in the twelfth century there were universal artists, but the problems of architecture were comparatively simple and uniform, and in sculpture and painting the matter was of more importance than the form. But in Italy at the time of the Renaissance, we find artists who in every branch created new and perfect works, and who also made the greatest impression as men. Others, outside the arts they practised, were masters of a vast circle of spiritual interests. . . .

The fifteenth century is, above all, that of the many-sided men. There is no biography which does not, besides the chief work of its hero, speak of other pursuits all passing beyond the limits of dilettantism. The Florentine merchant and statesman was often learned in both the classical languages; the most famous humanists read the ethics and politics of Aristotle to him and his sons; even the daughters of the house were highly educated. It is in these circles that private education was first treated seriously. The humanist, on his side, was compelled to the most varied attainments, since his philological learning was not limited, as it now is, to the theoretical knowledge of classical antiquity, but had to serve the practical needs of daily life. While studying Pliny, he made collections of natural history; the geography of the ancients was his guide in treating of modern geography, their history was his pattern in writing contemporary chronicles, even when composed in Italian; he not only translated the comedies of Plautus, but acted as manager when they were put on the stage; every effective form of ancient literature down to the dialogues of Lucian he did his best to imitate; and besides all this, he acted as magistrate, secretary, and diplomatist — not always to his own advantage.

But among these many-sided men, some who may truly be called all-sided, tower above the rest. Before analyzing the general phases of life and culture of this period, we may here, on the threshold of the fifteenth century, consider for a moment the figure of one of these giants — Leon Battista Alberti (b. 1404? d. 1472). His biography, which is only a fragment, speaks of him but little as an artist, and makes no mention at all of his great significance in the history of architecture. We shall now see what he was, apart from these special claims to distinction.

In all by which praise is won, Leon Battista was from his childhood the first. Of his various gymnastic feats and exercises we read with astonishment how, with his feet together, he could spring over a man's head; how, in the cathedral, he threw a coin in the air till it was heard to ring against the distant roof; how the wildest horses trembled under him. In three things he desired to appear faultless to others, in walking, in riding, and in speaking. He learned music without a master, and yet his compositions were admired by professional judges. Under the pressure of poverty, he studied both civil and canonical law for many years, till exhaustion brought on a severe illness. In his twenty-fourth year, finding his memory for words weakened, but his sense of facts unimpaired, he set to work at physics and mathematics. And all the while he acquired every sort of accomplishment and dexterity, cross-examining artists, scholars, and artisans of all descriptions, down to the cobblers, about the secrets and peculiarities of their craft. Painting and modelling he practised by the way, and especially excelled in admirable likenesses from memory. Great admiration was excited by his mysterious "camera obscura," in which he showed at one time the stars and the moon rising over rocky hills, at another wide landscapes with mountains and gulfs receding into dim perspective, and with fleets advancing on the waters in shade or sunshine. And that which others created he welcomed joyfully, and held every human achievement which followed the laws of beauty for something almost divine. To all this must be added his literary works, first of all those on art, which are landmarks and authorities of the first order for the Renaissance of Form, especially in architecture; then his Latin prose writings — novels and other works — of which some have been taken for productions of antiquity; his elegies, eclogues, and humorous dinner-speeches.

He also wrote an Italian treatise on domestic life in four books; various moral, philosophical, and historical works; and many speeches and poems, including a funeral oration on his dog. . . . His serious and witty sayings were thought worth collecting, and specimens of them, many columns long, are quoted in his biography. And all that he had and knew he imparted, as rich natures always do, without the least reserve, giving away his chief discoveries for nothing. But the deepest spring of his nature has yet to be spoken of — the sympathetic intensity with which he entered into the whole life around him. At the sight of noble trees and waving corn-fields he shed tears; handsome and dignified old men he honored as "a delight of nature," and could never look at them enough. Perfectly-formed animals won his goodwill as being specially favored by nature; and more than once, when he was ill, the sight of a beautiful landscape cured him. No wonder that those who saw him in this close and mysterious communion with the world ascribed to him the gift of prophecy. He was said to have foretold a bloody catastrophe in the family of Este, the fate of Florence, and the death of the Popes years before they happened, and to be able to read into the countenances and the hearts of men. It need not be added that an iron will pervaded and sustained his whole personality; like all the great men of the Renaissance, he said, "Men can do all things if they will."

And Leonardo da Vinci was to Alberti as the finisher to the beginner, as the master to the *dilettante*. Would only that Vasari's work were here supplemented by a description like that of Alberti! The colossal outlines of Leonardo's nature can never be more than dimly and distantly conceived.

The Modern Idea of Fame

To this inward development of the individual corresponds a new sort of outward distinction — the modern form of glory.

In other countries of Europe the different classes of society lived apart, each with its own mediaeval caste sense of honor. The poetical fame of the Troubadours and Minnesänger was peculiar to the knightly order. But in Italy social equality had appeared before the time of the tyrannies or the democracies. We there find early traces of a general society, having, as will be shown more fully later on, a common ground in Latin and Italian literature; and such a ground was needed for this new element in life to grow in. To this must be added that the Roman authors, who were now zealously studied, and especially Cicero, the most read and admired of all, are filled and saturated with the conception of fame, and that their subject itself — the universal empire of Rome — stood as a permanent ideal before the minds of Italians. From henceforth all the aspirations and achievements of the people were governed by a moral postulate, which was still unknown elsewhere in Europe. . . .

THE REVIVAL OF ANTIQUITY

Introducing Remarks

Now that this point in our historical view of Italian civilization has been reached, it is time to speak of the influence of antiquity, the "new birth" of which has been one-sidedly chosen as the name to sum up the whole period. The conditions which have been hitherto described would have sufficed, apart from antiquity, to upturn and to mature the national mind; and most of the intellectual tendencies which yet remain to be noticed would be conceivable without it. But both what has gone before and what we have still to discuss are colored in a thousand ways by the influence of the ancient world; and though the essence of the phenomena might still have been the same without the classical revival, it is only with and through this revival that they are actually manifested to us. The Renaissance would not have been the process of world-wide significance which it is, if its elements could be so easily separated from one another. We must insist upon it, as one of the chief propositions of this book, that it was not the revival of antiquity alone, but its union with the genius of the Italian people, which achieved the conquest of the Western world. The amount of independence which the national spirit maintained in this union varied according to circumstances. In the modern Latin literature of the period, it is very small, while in plastic art, as well as in other spheres, it is remarkably great; and hence the alliance between two distant epochs in the civilization of the same people, because concluded on equal terms, proved justifiable and fruitful. The rest of Europe was free either to repel or else partly or wholly to accept the mighty impulse which came forth from Italy. Where the latter was the case we may as well be spared the complaints over the early decay of mediaeval faith and civilization. Had these been strong enough to hold their ground, they would be alive to this day. If those elegiac natures which long to see them return could pass but one hour in the midst of them, they would gasp to be back in the modern air. That in a great historical process of this kind flowers of exquisite beauty may perish, without being made immortal in poetry or tradition, is undoubtedly true; nevertheless, we cannot wish the process undone. The general result of it consists in this — that by the side of the Church which had hitherto held the countries of the West together (though it was unable to do so much longer) there arose a new spiritual influence which, spreading itself abroad from Italy, became the breath of life for all the more instructed minds in Europe. The worst that can be said of the movement is, that it was antipopular, that through it Europe became for the first time sharply divided into the cultivated and uncultivated classes. The reproach will appear groundless when we reflect that even now the fact, though clearly recognized, cannot be altered. The separation, too, is by no means so cruel and absolute in Italy as elsewhere. The most artistic of her poets, Tasso, is in the hands of even the poorest.

The civilization of Greece and Rome, which, ever since the fourteenth century, obtained so powerful a hold on Italian life, as the source and basis of culture, as the object and ideal of existence, partly also as an avowed reaction against preceding tendencies — this civilization had long been exerting a partial influence on mediaeval Europe, even beyond the boundaries of Italy. The culture of which Charles the Great was a representative was, in the face of the barbarism of the seventh and eighth centuries, essentially a Renaissance, and could appear under no other form. Just as in the Romanesque architecture of the North, beside the general outlines inherited from antiquity, remarkable direct imitations of the antique also occur, so too monastic scholarship had not only gradually absorbed an immense mass of materials from Roman writers, but the style of it, from the days of Eginhard onwards, shows traces of conscious imitations.

But the resuscitation of antiquity took a different form in Italy from that which it assumed in the North. The wave of barbarism had scarcely gone by before the people, in whom the former life was but half effaced, showed a consciousness of its past and a wish to reproduce it. Elsewhere in Europe men deliberately and with reflection borrowed this or the other element of classical civilization; in Italy the sympathies both of the learned and of the people were naturally engaged on the side of antiquity as a whole, which stood to them as a symbol of past greatness. The Latin language, too, was easy to an Italian, and the numerous monuments and documents in which the country abounded facilitated a return to the past. With this tendency other elements — the popular character which time had now greatly modified, the political institutions imported by the Lombards from Germany, chivalry and other northern forms of civilization, and the influence of religion and the Church — combined to produce the modern Italian spirit, which was destined to serve as the model and ideal for the whole western world. . . .

But the great and general enthusiasm of the Italians for classical antiquity did not display itself before the fourteenth century. For this a development of civic life was required, which took place only in Italy, and there not till then. It was needful that noble and burger should first learn to dwell together on equal terms, and that a social world should arise which felt the want of culture, and had the leisure and the means to obtain it. But culture, as soon as it freed itself from the fantastic bonds of the Middle Ages, could not at once and without help find its way to the understanding of the physical and intellectual world. It needed a guide, and found one in the ancient civilization, with its wealth of truth and knowledge in every spiritual interest. Both the form and the substance of this civilization were adopted with admiring gratitude; it became the chief part of the culture of the age. The general condition of the country was favorable to this transformation. The mediaeval empire, since the fall of the Hohenstaufen, had either renounced, or was unable to make good, its claims on Italy. The Popes had migrated to Avignon. Most of the political powers actually in existence owed their origin to violent and illegitimate means. The spirit of the people, now awakened to self-consciousness, sought for some new and stable ideal on which to rest. And thus the vision of the world-wide empire of Italy and Rome so possessed the popular mind, that Cola di Rienzi could actually attempt to put it in practice. The conception he formed of his task, particularly when tribune for the first time, could only end in some extravagant comedy; nevertheless, the memory of ancient Rome was no slight support to the national sentiment. Armed afresh with its culture, the Italian soon felt himself in truth citizen of the most advanced nation in the world. . . .

Humanism in the Fourteenth Century

Who now were those who acted as mediators between their own age and a venerated antiquity, and made the latter a chief element in the culture of the former?

They were a crowd of the most miscellaneous sort, wearing one face today and another tomorrow; but they clearly felt themselves, and it was fully recognized by their time, that they formed a wholly new element in society. The "clerici vagantes" of the twelfth century, whose poetry we have already referred to, may perhaps be taken as their forerunners — the same unstable existence, the same free and more than free views of life, and the germs at all events of the same pagan tendencies in their poetry. But now, as competitor with the whole culture of the Middle Ages, which was essentially clerical and was fostered by the Church, there appeared a new civilization, founding itself on that which lay on the other side of the Middle Ages. Its active representatives became influential because they knew what the ancients knew, because they tried to write as the ancients wrote, because they began to think, and soon to feel, as the ancients thought and felt. The traditions to which they devoted themselves passed at a thousand points into genuine reproduction.

Some modern writers deplore the fact that the germs of a far more independent and essentially national culture, such as appeared in Florence about the year 1300, were afterwards so completely swamped by the humanists. There was then, we are told, nobody in Florence who could not read; even the donkey-men sang the verses of Dante; the best Italian manuscripts which we possess belonged originally to Florentine artisans; the publication of a popular encyclopaedia, like the "Tesoro" of Brunetto Latini, was then possible; and all this was founded on a strength and soundness of character due to the universal participation in public affairs, to commerce and travel, and to the systematic reprobation of idleness. The Florentines, it is urged, were at that time respected and influential throughout the whole world, and were called in that year, not without reason, by Pope Boniface VIII, "the fifth element." The rapid progress of humanism after the year 1400 paralyzed native impulses. Henceforth men looked to antiquity only for the solution of every problem, and consequently allowed literature to sink into mere quotation. Nay, the very fall of civil freedom is partly to be ascribed to all this, since the new learning rested on obedience to authority, sacrificed municipal rights to Roman law, and thereby both sought and found the favor of the despots.

These charges will occupy us now and then at a later stage of our inquiry, when we shall attempt to reduce them to their true value, and to weigh the losses against the gains of this movement. For the present we must confine ourselves to showing how the civilization even of the vigorous fourteenth century necessarily prepared the way for the complete victory of humanism, and how precisely the greatest representatives of the national Italian spirit were themselves the men who opened wide the gate for the measureless devotion to antiquity in the fifteenth century. . . .

THE DISCOVERY OF THE WORLD AND OF MAN

Journeys of the Italians

Freed from the countless bonds which elsewhere in Europe checked progress, having reached a high degree of individual development and been schooled by the teachings of antiquity, the Italian mind now turned to the discovery of the outward universe, and to the representation of it in speech and in form.

On the journeys of the Italians to distant parts of the world, we can here make but a few general observations. The crusades had opened unknown distances to the European mind, and awakened in all the passion for travel and adventure. It may be hard to indicate precisely the point where this passion allied itself with, or became the servant of, the thirst for knowledge; but it was in Italy that this was first and most completely the case. Even in the crusades the interest of the Italians was wider than that of other nations, since they already were a naval power and had commercial relations with the East. From time immemorial the Mediterranean sea had given to the nations that dwelt on its shores mental impulses different from those which governed the peoples of the North; and never, from the very structure of their character, could the Italians be adventurers in the sense which the word bore among the Teutons. After they were once at home in all the eastern harbours of the Mediterranean, it was natural that the most enterprising among them should be led to join that vast international movement of the Mohammedans which there found its outlet. A new half of the world lay, as it were, freshly discovered before them. Or, like Polo of Venice, they were caught in the current of the Mongolian peoples, and carried on to the steps of the throne of the Great Khan. At an early period, we find Italians sharing in the discoveries made in the Atlantic ocean; it was the Genoese who, in the thirteenth century, found the Canary Islands. In the same year, 1291, when Ptolemais, the last remnant of the Christian East, was lost, it was again the Genoese who made the first known attempt to find a sea-passage to the East Indies. Columbus himself is but the greatest of a long list of Italians who, in the service of the western nations, sailed into distant seas. The true discoverer, however, is not the man who first chances to stumble upon anything, but the man who finds what he has sought. Such a one alone stands in a link with the thoughts and interests of his predecessors, and this relationship will also determine the account he gives of his search. For which reason the Italians, although their claim to be the first comers on this or that shore may be disputed, will yet retain their title to be pre-eminently the nation of discoverers for the whole latter part of the Middle Ages. The fuller proof of this assertion belongs to the special history of discoveries. Yet ever and again we turn with admiration to the august figure of the great Genoese, by whom a new continent beyond the ocean was demanded, sought, and found; and who was the first to be able to say: "il mondo è poco" — the world is not so large as men have thought. At the time when Spain gave Alexander VI to the Italians, Italy gave Columbus to the Spaniards. Only a few weeks before the death of that pope (July 7th, 1503), Columbus wrote from Jamaica his noble letter to the thankless Catholic kings, which the ages to come can never read without profound emotion. In a codicil to his will, dated Valladolid, May 4th, 1506, he bequeathed to "his beloved home, the Republic of Genoa, the prayer-book which Pope Alexander had given him, and which in prison, in conflict, and in every kind of adversity had been to him the greatest of comforts." It seems as if these words cast upon the abhorred name of Borgia one last gleam of grace and mercy.

The development of geographical and the allied sciences among the Italians must, like the history of their voyages, be touched upon but very briefly. A superficial comparison of their achievements with those of other nations shows an early and striking superiority on their part. Where, in the middle of the fifteenth century, could be found, anywhere but in Italy, such a union of geographical, statistical, and historical knowledge as was found in Aeneas Sylvius? Not only in his great geographical work, but in his letters and commentaries, he describes with equal mastery landscapes, cities, manners, industries and products, political conditions and constitutions, wherever he can use his own observation or the evidence of eye-witnesses. What he takes from books is naturally of less moment. Even the short sketch of that valley in the Tyrolese Alps, where Frederick III had given him a benefice, and still more his description of Scotland, leaves untouched none of the relations of human life, and displays a power and method of unbiased observation and comparison impossible in any but a countryman of Columbus, trained in the school of the ancients. Thousands saw and, in part, knew what he did, but they felt no impulse to draw a picture of it, and were unconscious that the world desired such pictures.

In geography as in other matters, it is vain to attempt to distinguish how much is to be attributed to the study of the ancients, and how much to the special genius of the Italians. They saw and treated the things of this world from an objective point of view, even before they were familiar with the ancient literature, partly because they were themselves a half-ancient people, and partly because their political circumstances predisposed them to it; but they would not so rapidly have attained to such perfection had not the old geographers showed them the way. The influence of the existing Italian geographies on the spirit and tendencies of the travellers and discoverers was also inestimable. Even the simple "dilettante" of a science — if in the present case we should assign to Aeneas Sylvius so low a rank — can diffuse just that sort of general interest in the subject which prepares for new pioneers the indispensable groundwork of a favorable predisposition in the public mind. True discoverers in any science know well what they owe to such mediation.

Natural Science in Italy

For the position of the Italians in the sphere of the natural sciences, we must refer the reader to the special treatises on the subject, of which the only one with which we are familiar is the superficial and depreciatory work of Libri. The dispute as to the priority of particular discoveries concerns us all the less, since we hold that, at any time, and among any civilized people, a man may appear who, starting with very scanty preparation, is driven by an irresistible impulse into the path of scientific investigation, and through his native gifts achieves the most astonishing success. Such men were Gerbert of Rheims and Roger Bacon. That they were masters of the whole knowledge of the age in their several departments was a natural consequence of the spirit in which they worked. When once the veil of illusion was torn asunder, when once the dread of nature and the slavery to books and tradition were overcome, countless problems lay before them for solution. It is another matter when a whole people takes a natural delight in the study and investigation of nature, at a time when other nations are indifferent, that is to say, when the discoverer is not threatened or wholly ignored, but can count on the friendly support of congenial spirits. That this was the case in Italy, is unquestionable. The Italian students of nature trace with pride in the "Divine Comedy" the hints and proofs of Dante's scientific interest in nature. On his claim to priority in this or that discovery or reference, we must leave the men of science to decide; but every layman must be struck by the wealth of his observations on the external world, shown merely in his pictures and comparisons. He, more than any other modern poet, takes them from reality, whether in nature or human life, and uses them, never as mere ornament, but in order to give the reader the fullest and most adequate sense of his meaning. It is in astronomy that he appears chiefly as a scientific specialist, though it must not be forgotten that many astronomical allusions in his great poem, which now appear to us learned, must then have been intelligible to the general reader. Dante, learning apart, appeals to a popular knowledge of the heavens, which the Italians of his day, from the mere fact that they were nautical people, had in common with the ancients. This knowledge of the rising and setting of the constellations has been rendered superfluous to the modern world by calendars and clocks, and with it has gone whatever interest in astronomy the people may once have had. Nowadays, with our schools and handbooks, every child knows — what Dante did not know — that the earth moves round the sun; but the interest once taken in the subject itself has given place, except in the case of astronomical specialists, to the most absolute indifference.

The pseudo-science, which also dealt with the stars, proves nothing against the inductive spirit of the Italians of that day. That spirit was but crossed, and at times overcome, by the passionate desire to penetrate the future. We shall recur to the subject of astrology when we come to speak of the moral and religious character of the people.

The Church treated this and other pseudo-sciences nearly always with toleration; and showed itself actually hostile even to genuine science only when a charge of heresy together with necromancy was also in question — which certainly was often the case. A point which it would be interesting to decide is this: whether, and in what cases, the Dominican (and also the Franciscan) Inquisitors in Italy were conscious of the falsehood of the charges, and yet condemned the accused, either to oblige some enemy of the prisoner or from hatred to natural science, and particularly to experiments. The latter doubtless occurred, but it is not easy to prove the fact. What helped to cause such persecutions in the North, namely, the opposition made to the innovators by the upholders of the received official, scholastic system of nature, was of little or no weight in Italy. Pietro of Albano, at the beginning of the fourteenth century, is well known to have fallen a victim to the envy of another physician, who accused him before the Inquisition of heresy and magic; and something of the same kind may have happened in the case of his Paduan contemporary, Giovannino Sanguinacci, who was known as an innovator in medical practice. He escaped, however, with banishment. Nor must it be forgotten that the inquisitorial power of the Dominicans was exercised less uniformly in Italy than in the North. Tyrants and free cities in the fourteenth century treated the clergy at times with such sovereign contempt, that very different matters from natural science went unpunished. But when, with the fifteenth century, antiquity became the leading power in Italy, the breach it made in the old system was turned to account by every branch of secular science. Humanism, nevertheless, attracted to itself the best strength of the nation, and thereby, no doubt, did injury to the inductive investigation of nature. Here and there the Inquisition suddenly started into life, and punished or burned physicians as blasphemers or magicians. In such cases it is hard to discover what was the true motive underlying the condemnation. And after all, Italy, at the close of the fifteenth century, with Paolo Toscanelli, Luca Pacciolo and Leonardo da Vinci, held incomparably the highest place among European nations in mathematics and the natural sciences, and the learned men of every country, even Regiomontanus and Copernicus, confessed themselves its pupils.

A significant proof of the wide-spread interest in natural history is found in the zeal which showed itself at an early period for the collection and comparative study of plants and animals. Italy claims to be the first creator of botanical gardens, though possibly they may have served a chiefly practical end, and the claim to priority may be itself disputed. It is of far greater importance that princes and wealthy men in laying out their pleasure-gardens, instinctively made a point of collecting the greatest possible number of different plants in all their species and varieties. Thus in the fifteenth century the noble grounds of the Medicean Villa Careggi appear from the descriptions we have of them to have been almost a botanical garden, with countless specimens of different trees and shrubs. Of the same kind was a villa of the Cardinal Trivulzio, at the beginning of the sixteenth century, in the Roman Campagna towards Tivoli, with hedges made up of various species of roses, with trees of every description — the fruit-trees especially showing an astonishing variety — with twenty different sorts of vines and a large kitchen-garden. This is evidently something very different from the score or two of familiar medicinal plants, which were to be found in the garden of any castle or monastery in Western Europe. Along with a careful cultivation of fruit for the purposes of the table, we find an interest in the plant for its own sake, on account of the pleasure it gives to the eye. We learn

from the history of art at how late a period this passion for botanical collections was laid aside, and gave place to what was considered the picturesque style of landscape-gardening.

The collections, too, of foreign animals not only gratified curiosity, but served also the higher purposes of observation. The facility of transport from the southern and eastern harbours of the Mediterranean, and the mildness of the Italian climate, made it practicable to buy the largest animals of the south, or to accept them as presents from the Sultans. The cities and princes were especially anxious to keep live lions, even when the lion was not, as in Florence, the emblem of the State. The lions' den was generally in or near the government palace, as in Perugia and Florence; in Rome, it lay on the slope of the Capitol. The beasts sometimes served as executioners of political judgments, and no doubt, apart from this, they kept alive a certain terror in the popular mind. Their condition was also held to be ominous of good or evil. Their fertility, especially, was considered a sign of public prosperity, and no less a man than Giovanni Villani thought it worth recording that he was present at the delivery of a lioness. The cubs were often given to allied states and princes, or to Condottieri, as a reward of valor. In addition to the lions, the Florentines began very early to keep leopards, for which a special keeper was appointed. Borso of Ferrara used to set his lions to fight with bulls, bears, and wild boars.

By the end of the fifteenth century, however, true menageries (serragli), now reckoned part of the suitable appointments of a court, were kept by many of the princes. "It belongs to the position of the great," says Matarazzo, "to keep horses, dogs, mules, falcons, and other birds, court-jesters, singers, and foreign animals." The menagerie at Naples, in the time of Ferrante and others, contained a giraffe and a zebra, presented, it seems, by the ruler of Baghdad. Filippo Maria Visconti possessed not only horses which cost him each 500 or

1,000 pieces of gold, and valuable English dogs, but a number of leopards brought from all parts of the East; the expense of his hunting-birds which were collected from the countries of Northern Europe, amounted to 3,000 pieces of gold a month. "The Cremonese say that the Emperor Frederick II brought an elephant into their city, sent him from India by Prester John," we read in Brunetto Latini; Petrarch records the dying out of the elephants in Italy. King Emanuel the Great of Portugal knew well what he was about when he presented Leo X with an elephant and a rhinoceros. It was under such circumstances that the foundations of a scientific zoology and botany were laid.

A practical fruit of these zoological studies was the establishment of studs, of which the Mantuan, under Francesco Gonzaga, was esteemed the first in Europe. An interest in, and knowledge of the different breeds of horses is as old, no doubt, as riding itself, and the crossing of the European with the Asiatic must have been common from the time of the crusades. In Italy, a special inducement to perfect the breed was offered by the prizes at the horse-races held in every considerable town in the peninsula. In the Mantuan stables were found the infallible winners in these contests, as well as the best military chargers, and the horses best suited by their stately appearance for presents to great people. Gonzaga kept stallions and mares from Spain, Ireland, Africa, Thrace, and Cilicia, and for the sake of the last he cultivated the friendship of the Sultan. All possible experiments were here tried, in order to produce the most perfect animals.

Even human menageries were not wanting. The famous Cardinal Ippolito Medici, bastard of Giuliano, Duke of Nemours, kept at his strange court a troop of barbarians who talked no less than twenty different languages, and who were all of them perfect specimens of their races. Among them were incomparable *voltigeurs* of the best blood of the North African Moors, Tartar bowmen, Negro wrestlers,

Indian divers, and Turks, who generally accompanied the Cardinal on his hunting expeditions. When he was overtaken by an early death (1535), this motley band carried the corpse on their shoulders from Itri to Rome, and mingled with the general mourning for the open-handed Cardinal their medley of tongues and violent gesticulations.

These scattered notices of the relations of the Italians to natural science, and their interest in the wealth and variety of the products of nature, are only fragments of a great subject. No one is more conscious than the author of the defects in his knowledge on this point. Of the multitude of special works in which the subject is adequately treated, even the names are but imperfectly known to him. . . .

The Discovery of Man

To the discovery of the outward world the Renaissance added a still greater achievement, by first discerning and bringing to light the full, whole nature of man.

This period, as we have seen, first gave the highest development to individuality, and then led the individual to the most zealous and thorough study of himself in all forms and under all conditions. Indeed, the development of personality is essentially involved in the recognition of it in oneself and in others. Between these two great processes our narrative has placed the influence of ancient literature, because the mode of conceiving and representing both the individual and human nature in general was defined and colored by that influence. But the power of conception and representation lay in the age and in the people.

The facts which we shall quote in evidence of our thesis will be few in number. Here, if anywhere in the course of this discussion, the author is conscious that he is treading on the perilous ground of conjecture, and that what seems to him a clear, if delicate and gradual, transition in the intellectual movement of the fourteenth and fifteenth centuries, may not be equally plain to others. The gradual awakening of the souls of a people is a phenomenon which may produce a different impression on each spectator. Time will judge which impression is the most faithful.

Happily the study of the intellectual side of human nature began, not with the search after a theoretical psychology — for that, Aristotle still sufficed — but with the endeavor to observe and to describe. The indispensable ballast of theory was limited to the popular doctrine of the four temperaments, in its then habitual union with the belief in the influence of the planets. Such conceptions may remain ineradicable in the minds of individuals, without hindering the general progress of the age. It certainly makes on us a singular impression, when we meet them at a time when human nature in its deepest essence and in all its characteristic expressions was not only known by exact observation, but represented by an immortal poetry and art. It sounds almost ludicrous when an otherwise competent observer considers Clement VII to be of a melancholy temperament, but defers his judgment to that of the physicians, who declare the Pope of a sanguine-choleric nature; or when we read that the same Gaston de Foix, the victor of Ravenna, whom Giorgione painted and Bambaia carved, and whom all the historians describe, had the saturnine temperament. No doubt those who use these expressions mean something by them; but the terms in which they tell us their meaning are strangely out of date in the Italy of the sixteenth century. . . .

Even apart from the "Divine Comedy," Dante would have marked by these youthful poems the boundary between mediaevalism and modern times. The human spirit had taken a mighty step towards the consciousness of its own secret life.

The revelations in this matter which are contained in the "Divine Comedy" itself are simply immeasurable; and it would be necessary to go through the whole poem, one canto after another, in order to do justice to its value from this point of view. Happily we have no need to do this, as it

has long been a daily food of all the countries of the West. Its plan, and the ideas on which it is based, belong to the Middle Ages, and appeal to our interest only historically; but it is nevertheless the beginning of all modern poetry, through the power and richness shown in the description of human nature in every shape and attitude.

From this time forwards poetry may have experienced unequal fortunes, and may show, for half a century together, a so-called relapse. But its nobler and more vital principle was saved for ever; and whenever in the fourteenth, fifteenth, and in the beginning of the sixteenth centuries, an original mind devotes himself to it, he represents a more advanced stage than any poet out of Italy, given — what is certainly not always easy to settle satisfactorily — an equality of natural gifts to start with.

Here, as in other things in Italy, culture — to which poetry belongs — precedes the plastic arts and, in fact, gives them their chief impulse. More than a century elapsed before the spiritual element in painting and sculpture attained a power of expression in any way analogous to that of the "Divine Comedy." How far the same rule holds good for the artistic development of other nations, and of what importance the whole question may be, does not concern us here. For Italian civilization it is of decisive weight. . . .

That the ancient poets, particularly the elegists, and Virgil, in the fourth book of the Aeneid, were not without influence on the Italians of this and the following generation is beyond a doubt; but the spring of sentiment within the latter was nevertheless powerful and original. If we compare them in this respect with their contemporaries in other countries, we shall find in them the earliest complete expression of modern European feeling. The question, be it remembered, is not to know whether eminent men of other nations did not feel as deeply and as nobly, but who first gave documentary proof of the widest knowledge of the movements of the human heart. . . .

The Equalization of Classes

Every period of civilization which forms a complete and consistent whole, manifests itself not only in political life, in religion, art, and science, but also sets its characteristic stamp on social life. Thus the Middle Ages had their courtly and aristocratic manners and etiquette, differing but little in the various countries of Europe, as well as their peculiar forms of middle-class life.

Italian customs at the time of the Renaissance offer in these respects the sharpest contrast to mediaevalism. The foundation on which they rest is wholly different. Social intercourse in its highest and most perfect form now ignored all distinctions of caste, and was based simply on the existence of an educated class as we now understand the word. Birth and origin were without influence, unless combined with leisure and inherited wealth. Yet this assertion must not be taken in an absolute and unqualified sense, since mediaeval distinctions still sometimes made themselves felt to a greater or less degree, if only as a means of maintaining equality with the aristocratic pretensions of the less advanced countries of Europe. But the main current of the time went steadily towards the fusion of classes in the modern sense of the phrase.

The fact was of vital importance that, from certainly the twelfth century onwards, the nobles and the burghers dwelt together within the walls of the cities. The interests and pleasures of both classes were thus identified, and the feudal lord learned to look at society from another point of view than that of his mountain castle. The Church, too, in Italy never suffered itself, as in northern countries, to be used as a means of providing for the younger sons of noble families. Bishoprics, abbacies, and canonries were often given from the most unworthy motives, but still not according to the pedigrees of the applicants; and if the bishops in Italy were more numerous, poorer, and, as a rule, destitute of all sovereign rights, they still lived in the cities where their cathedrals stood, and formed, together with their chapters, an important element in the cultivated society of the place. In the age of despots and absolute princes which followed, the nobility in most of the cities had the motives and the leisure to give themselves up to a private life free from the political danger and adorned with all that was elegant and enjoyable, but at the same time hardly distinguishable from that of the wealthy burgher. And after the time of Dante, when the new poetry and literature were in the hands of all Italy, when to this was added the revival of ancient culture and the new interest in man as such, when the successful Condottiere became a prince, and not only good birth, but legitimate birth, ceased to be indispensable for a throne, it might well seem that the age of equality had dawned, and the belief in nobility vanished for ever.

From a theoretical point of view, when the appeal was made to antiquity, the conception of nobility could be both justified and condemned from Aristotle alone. Dante, for example, adapts from Aristotelian definition, "Nobility rests on excellence and inherited wealth," his own saying, "Nobility rests on personal excellence or on that of predecessors." But elsewhere he is not satisfied with this conclusion. He blames himself, because even in Paradise, while talking with his ancestor Cacciaguida, he made mention of his noble origin, which is but a mantle from which time is ever cutting something away, unless we ourselves add daily fresh worth to it. And in the "Convito" he disconnects "nobile" and "nobiltà" from every condition of birth, and identifies the idea with the capacity for moral and intellectual eminence, laying a special stress on high culture by calling "nobiltà" the sister of "filosofia."

And as time went on, the greater the influence of humanism on the Italian mind, the firmer and more widespread became the conviction that birth decides nothing as to the goodness or badness of a man. In the fifteenth century this was the prevailing opinion. Poggio, in his dialogue "On nobility," agrees with his interlocutors — Niccolò Niccoli, and Lorenzo Medici, brother of the great Cosimo — that there is no other nobility than that of personal merit. The keenest shafts of his ridicule are directed against much of what vulgar prejudice thinks indispensable to an aristocratic life. "A man is all the farther removed from true nobility, the longer his forefathers have plied the trade of brigands. The taste for hawking and hunting savors no more of nobility than the nests and lairs of the hunted creatures of spikenard. The cultivation of the soil, as practised by the ancients, would be much nobler than this senseless wandering through the hills and woods, by which men make themselves liker to the brutes than to the reasonable creatures. It may serve well enough as a recreation, but not as the business of a lifetime." The life of the English and French chivalry in the country or in the woody fastnesses seems to him thoroughly ignoble, and worst of all the doings of the robber-knights of Germany. Lorenzo here begins to take the part of the nobility, but not — which is characteristic — appealing to any natural sentiment in its favor, but because Aristotle in the fifth book of the "Politics" recognizes the nobility as existent, and defines it as resting on excellence and inherited wealth. To this Niccoli retorts that Aristotle gives this not as his own conviction, but as the popular impression; in his "Ethics," where he speaks as he thinks, he calls him noble who strives after that which is truly good. Lorenzo urges upon him vainly that the Greek word for nobility means good birth; Niccoli thinks the Roman word "nobilis" (i.e. remarkable) a better one, since it makes nobility depend on a man's deeds. Together with these discussions, we find a sketch of the conditions of the nobles in various parts of Italy. In Naples they will not work, and busy themselves neither with their own estates nor with trade and commerce, which they hold to be discreditable; they either loiter at home or ride about on horseback. The Roman nobility also despise trade, but farm their own property; the cultivation of

the land even opens the way to a title; "it is a respectable but boorish nobility." In Lombardy the nobles live upon the rent of their inherited estates; descent and the abstinence from any regular calling constitute nobility. In Venice, the "nobili," the ruling caste, were all merchants. Similarly in Genoa the nobles and non-nobles were alike merchants and sailors, and only separated by their birth; some few of the former, it is true, still lurked as brigands in their mountain-castles. In Florence a part of the old nobility had devoted themselves to trade; another, and certainly by far the smaller part, enjoyed the satisfaction of their titles, and spent their time, either in nothing at all, or else in hunting and hawking.

The decisive fact was, that nearly everywhere in Italy, even those who might be disposed to pride themselves on their birth could not make good the claims against the power of culture and of wealth, and that their privileges in politics and at court were not sufficient to encourage any strong feeling of caste. Venice offers only an apparent exception to this rule, for there the "nobili" led the same life as their fellow-citizens, and were distinguished by few honorary privileges. The case was certainly different at Naples, where the strict isolation and the ostentatious vanity of its nobility excluded, above all other causes, from the spiritual movement of the Renaissance. The traditions of mediaeval Lombardy and Normandy, and the French aristocratic influences which followed, all tended in this direction; and the Aragonese government, which was established by the middle of the fifteenth century, completed the work, and accomplished in Naples what followed a hundred years later in the rest of Italy — a social transformation in obedience to Spanish ideas, of which the chief features were the contempt for work and the passion for titles. The effect of this new influence was evident, even in the smaller towns, before the year 1500. We hear complaints from La Cava that the place had been proverbially rich, as long as it was filled with masons and weavers; whilst now, since instead of looms and trowels nothing but spurs, stirrups and gilded belts was to be seen, since everybody was trying to become Doctor of Laws or of Medicine, Notary, Officer or Knight, the most intolerable poverty prevailed. In Florence an analogous change appears to have taken place by the time of Cosimo, the first Grand Duke; he is thanked for adopting the young people, who now despise trade and commerce, as knights of his order of St. Stephen. This goes straight in the teeth of the good old Florentine custom, by which fathers left property to their children on the condition that they should have some occupation. But a mania for titles of a curious and ludicrous sort sometimes crossed and thwarted, especially among the Florentines, the levelling influence of art and culture. This was the passion for knighthood, which became one of the most striking follies of the day, at a time when the dignity itself had lost every shadow of significance.

MORALITY AND RELIGION

Morality

. . . If we now attempt to sum up the principal features in the Italian character of that time, as we know it from a study of the life of the upper classes, we shall obtain something like the following result. The fundamental vice of this character was at the same time a condition of its greatness, namely, excessive individualism. The individual first inwardly casts off the authority of a state which, as a fact, is in most cases tyrannical and illegitimate, and what he thinks and does is, rightly or wrongly, now called treason. The sight of victorious egotism in others drives him to defend his own right by his own arm. And, while thinking to restore his inward equilibrium, he falls, through the vengeance which he executes, into the hands of the powers of darkness. His love, too, turns mostly for satisfaction to another individuality equally developed, namely, to his neighbor's wife. In face of all objective facts, of laws and restraints of whatever kind, he retains the feeling of his own sovereignty, and in each single instance forms his decision independently, according as honor or interest, passion or calculation, revenge or renunciation, gain the upper hand in his own mind.

If therefore egotism in its wider as well as narrower sense is the root and fountain of all evil, the more highly developed Italian was for this reason more inclined to wickedness than the members of other nations of that time.

But this individual development did not come upon him through any fault of his own, but rather through an historical necessity. It did not come upon him alone, but also, and chiefly, by means of Italian culture, upon the other nations of Europe, and has constituted since then the higher atmosphere which they breathe. In itself it is neither good nor bad, but necessary; within it has grown up a modern standard of good and evil — a sense of moral responsibility — which is essentially different from that which was familiar to the Middle Ages.

But the Italian of the Renaissance had to bear the first mighty surging of a new age. Through his gifts and his passions, he has become the most characteristic representative of all the heights and all the depths of his time. By the side of profound corruption appeared human personalities of the noblest harmony, and an artistic splendor which shed upon the life of man a lustre which neither antiquity nor mediaevalism either could or would bestow upon it. . . .

Religion and the Spirit of the Renaissance

But in order to reach a definite conclusion with regard to the religious sense of the men of this period, we must adopt a different method. From their intellectual attitude in general, we can infer their relation both to the Divine idea and to the existing religion of their age.

These modern men, the representatives of the culture of Italy, were born with the same religious instincts as other mediaeval Europeans. But their powerful individuality made them in religion, as in other matters, altogether subjective, and the intense charm which the discovery of the inner and outer universe exercised upon them rendered them markedly worldly. In the rest of Europe religion remained, till a much later period, something given from without, and in practical life egotism and sensuality alternated with devotion and repentance. The latter had no spiritual competitors, as in Italy, or only to a far smaller extent.

Further, the close and frequent relations of Italy with Byzantium and the Mohammedan peoples, had produced a dispassionate tolerance which weakened the ethnographical conception of a privileged Christendom. And when classical antiquity with its men and institutions became an ideal of life, as well as the greatest of historical memories, ancient speculation and scepticism obtained in many cases a complete mastery over the minds of Italians.

Since, again, the Italians were the first modern people of Europe who gave themselves boldly to speculations on freedom and necessity, and since they did so under violent and lawless political circumstances, in which evil seemed often to win a splendid and lasting victory, their belief in God began to waver, and their view of the government of the world became fatalistic. And when their passionate natures refused to rest in the sense of uncertainty, they made a shift to help themselves out with ancient, oriental, or mediaeval superstition. They took to astrology and magic.

Finally, these intellectual giants, these representatives of the Renaissance, show, in respect to religion, a quality which is common in youthful natures. Distinguishing keenly between good and evil, they yet are conscious of no sin. Every disturbance of their inward harmony they feel themselves able to make good out of the plastic resources of their own nature, and therefore they feel no repentance. The need of salvation thus becomes felt more and more dimly, while the ambitions and the intellectual activity of the present either shut out altogether every thought of a world to come, or else caused it to assume a poetic instead of a dogmatic form.

When we look on all this as pervaded and often perverted by the all-powerful Italian imagination, we obtain a picture of that time which is certainly more in accordance with truth than are vague declamations against modern paganism. And closer investigation often reveals to us that underneath this outward shell much genuine religion could still survive. . . .

That religion should again become an affair of the individual and of his own personal feeling was inevitable when the Church became corrupt in doctrine and tyrannous in practice, and is a proof that the European mind was still alive. It is true that this showed itself in many different ways. While the mystical and ascetical sects of the North lost no time in creating new outward forms for their new modes of thought and feeling, each individual in Italy went his own way, and thousands wandered on the sea of life without any religious guidance whatever. All the more must we admire those who attained and held fast to a personal religion. They were not to blame for being unable to have any part or lot in the old Church, as she then was; nor would it be reasonable to expect that they should all of them go through that mighty spiritual labor which was appointed to the German reformers. The form and aim of this personal faith, as it showed itself in the better minds, will be set forth at the close of our work.

The worldliness, through which the Renaissance seems to offer so striking a contrast to the Middle Ages, owed its first origin to the flood of new thoughts, purposes, and views, which transformed the mediaeval conception of nature and man. The spirit is not in itself more hostile to religion than that "culture" which now holds its place, but which can give us only a feeble notion of the universal ferment which the discovery of a new world of greatness then called forth. This worldliness was not frivolous, but earnest, and was ennobled by art and poetry. It is a lofty necessity of the modern spirit that this attitude, once gained, can never again be lost, that an irresistible impulse forces us to the investigation of men and things, and that we must hold this inquiry to be our proper end and work. How soon and by what paths this search will lead us back to God, and in what ways the religious temper of the individual will be affected by it, are questions which cannot be met by any general answer. The Middle Ages, which spared themselves the trouble of induction and free enquiry, can have no right to impose upon us their dogmatical verdict in a matter of such vast importance. . . .

Antiquity exercised an influence of another kind than that of Islam, and this not through its religion, which was but too much like the Catholicism of this period, but through its philosophy. Ancient literature now worshipped as something incomparable, is full of the victory of philosophy over religious tradition. An endless number of systems and fragments of systems were suddenly presented to the Italian mind, not as curiosities or even as heresies, but almost with the authority of dogmas, which had now to be reconciled rather than discriminated. In nearly all these various opinions and doctrines a certain kind of belief in God was implied; but taken altogether they formed a marked contrast to the Christian faith in a Divine government of the world. . . .

The fourteenth century was chiefly stimulated by the writings of Cicero, who, though in fact an eclectic, yet, by his habit of setting forth the opinions of different schools, without coming to a decision between them, exercised the influence of a sceptic. Next in importance came Seneca, and the few works of Aristotle which had been translated into Latin. The immediate fruit of these studies was the capacity to reflect on great subjects, if not in direct opposition to the authority of the Church, at all events independently of it.

In the course of the fifteenth century the works of antiquity were discovered and diffused with extraordinary rapidity. All the writings of the Greek philosophers which we ourselves possess were now, at least in the form of Latin translations, in everybody's hands. It is a curious fact that some of the most zealous apostles of this new culture were men of the strictest piety, or even ascetics. Fra Ambrogio Camaldolese, as a spiritual dignitary chiefly occupied with ecclesiastical affairs, and as a literary man with the translation of the Greek Fathers of the Church, could not repress the humanistic impulse, and at the request of Cosimo de' Medici, undertook to translate Diogenes Laertius into Latin. His contemporaries, Niccolò Nocoli, Giannozzo Mannetti, Donato Acciajuoli, and Pope Nicholas V, united to a many-sided humanism profound biblical scholarship and deep piety. In Vittorino da Feltre the same temper has been already noticed. The same Matthew Vegio, who added a thirteenth book to the "Aeneid," had an enthusiasm for the memory of St. Augustine and his mother Monica which cannot have been without a deeper influence upon him. The result of all these tendencies was that the Platonic Academy at Florence deliberately chose for its object the reconciliation of the spirit of antiquity with that of Christianity. It was a remarkable oasis in the humanism of the period.

This humanism was in fact pagan, and became more and more so as its sphere widened in the fifteenth century. Its representatives, whom we have already described as the advanced guard of an unbridled individualism, display as a rule such a character that even their religion, which is sometimes professed very definitely, becomes a matter of indifference to us. They easily got the name of atheists, if they showed themselves indifferent to religion, and spoke freely against the Church; but not one of them ever professed, or dared to profess, a formal, philosophical atheism. If they sought for any leading principle, it must have been a kind of superficial rationalism — a careless inference from the many and contradictory opinions of antiquity with which they busied themselves, and from the discredit into which the Church and her doctrines had fallen. This was the sort of reasoning which was near bringing Galeottus Martius to the stake, had not his former pupil Pope Sixtus IV, perhaps at the request of Lorenzo de' Medici, saved him from the hands of the Inquisition. Galeotto had ventured to write that the man who walked uprightly, and acted according to the natural law born within him, would go to heaven, whatever nation he belonged to. . . .

With respect to the moral government of the world, the humanists seldom get beyond a cold and resigned consideration of the prevalent violence and misrule. In this mood the many works "On Fate," or whatever name they bear, are written. They tell of the turning of the wheel of Fortune, and on the instability of earthly, especially political, things. Providence is only brought in because the writers would still be ashamed of undisguised fatalism, of the avowal of their ignorance, or of useless complaints. Gioviano Pontano ingeniously illustrates the nature of that mysterious something which men call Fortune by a hundred incidents, most of which belonged to his own experience. The subject is treated more humorously by Aeneas Sylvius, in the form of a vision seen in a dream. The aim of Poggio, on the other hand, in a work written in his old age, is to represent the world as a vale of tears, and to fix the happiness of various classes as low as possible. This tone became in future the prevalent one. Distinguished men drew up a debit and credit of the happiness and unhappiness of their lives, and generally found that the latter outweighed the former. . . .

But the way in which resuscitated antiquity affected religion most powerfully, was not through any doctrines or philosophical system, but through a general tendency which it fostered. The men, and in some respects the institutions of antiquity were preferred to those of the Middle Ages, and in the eager attempt to imitate and reproduce them, religion was left to take care of itself. All was absorbed in the admiration for historical greatness. To this the philologians added many special follies of their own, by which they became the mark for general attention. How far Paul II was justified in calling his Abbreviators and their friends to account for their paganism, is certainly a matter of great doubt, as his biographer and chief victim, Platina, has shown a masterly skill in explaining his vindictiveness on other grounds, and especially in making him play a ludicrous figure. The charges of infidelity, paganism, denial of immortality, and so forth, were not made against the accused till the charge of high treason had broken down. Paul, indeed, if we are correctly informed about him, was by no means the man to judge of intellectual things. He knew little Latin, and spoke Italian at Consistories and in diplomatic negotiations. It was he who exhorted the Romans to teach their children nothing beyond reading and writing. His priestly narrowness of views reminds us of Savonarola, with the difference that Paul might fairly have been told that he and his like were in great part to blame if culture made men hostile to religion. It cannot, nevertheless, be doubted that he felt a real anxiety about the pagan tendencies which surrounded him. And what, in truth, may not the humanists have allowed themselves at the court of the profligate pagan, Sigismondo Malatesta? How far these men, destitute for the most part of fixed principle, ventured to go, depended assuredly on the sort of influences they were exposed to. Nor could they treat of Christianity without paganizing it. . . .

MEDIAEVAL INSTITUTIONS IN THE MODERN WORLD

C. H. MCILWAIN

Charles Howard McIlwain was born in 1871 and has had a long and distinguished career. Emeritus professor of Harvard University since 1946, he inspired many generations of Harvard students with his brilliant and incisive lectures in his course in the history of political thought. Although his chief interest has been in the medieval period and he has written several notable works dealing with the political thought and institutions of this era, in 1924 he was awarded the Pulitzer Prize for his book on *The American Revolution: A Constitutional Interpretation.* In 1936 he was honored by being elected president of the American Historical Association.

I T IS a common fault, to which I suppose we are all more or less subject, when we are asked long in advance to speak on some topic, to accept gaily without counting the cost. It was in that spirit that I welcomed the honor but incurred the obligation of speaking to you today on the subject of the Mediaeval in the Modern. But when I set to work my troubles began. For before we dare speak of the mediaeval in the modern, we must know what we mean when we use the term "mediaeval"; and it is amazing what different pictures that word calls up for different minds . . .

. . . in the intellectual sphere, there is the view that the thirteenth century is, as it has been called, "the greatest of Christian centuries"; and, on the other hand, the notion, widespread a generation ago if not now, that the Renaissance was a "rediscovery of the world and of men." What shall we believe about that? For these two views are irreconcilable. No doubt historians as far removed from our time as we are from the Middle Ages will have somewhat the same conflicting opinions about the first half of the twentieth century. Even today we find some saying that these moving times are a great time to be alive, while others can only look back with longing to an earlier period when rights and honor and oaths were at least respected, even if not always observed.

With such a disparity of opinions about the present, how can we be surprised to find them in regard to the Middle Ages? Our definitions of the mediaeval, like those of the present, will be affected by our temperament, our traditions, and our peculiar studies. The best definition we can frame will be partial, incomplete, and inadequate; and the sum of all these defects will probably be the result of ignorance of something essential. . . .

The period that we dub mediaeval is a long one, and on that side of it in which my own studies have lain I think we find, within the period itself, changes as profound, if not even more profound, than those which mark off our modern institutions from the ones we call mediaeval. In the field of political institutions and ideas I venture to think that what Professor

From C. H. McIlwain, "Mediaeval Institutions in the Modern World," in *Speculum,* XVI (1941), 275–283. By permission of the Mediaeval Academy of America.

Haskins has termed "the Renaissance of the twelfth century" marks a more fundamental change than the later developments to which we usually attach the word "Renaissance"; that the constitutionalism of the modern world owes as much, if not even more, to the twelfth and the thirteenth centuries than to any later period of comparable length before the seventeenth.

All this is to do little more than say that the term "Middle Ages" in its widest extent is a term which includes institutions and ideas as widely different from each other as the so-called mediaeval is from the modern. If so, which of them shall we term "mediaeval" *par excellence?* Or shall we give it all up, and say that all we dare do is to term "mediaeval" anything and everything we find in the whole millenium generally included under the phrase "Middle Ages"? Pitfalls certainly do lie in the path of anyone who is looking for the peculiar flavor of the Middle Ages, and many there are who have fallen in. In my own field I am thinking particularly of historians such as Freeman, who became so obsessed by the notion of constitutional liberty as the dominant note of mediaeval political life that he could never see the feudalism that everywhere stared him in the face, or, if he saw it, could only damn it as an abuse. He had a pattern ready-made to which the institutions of the time must conform.

There have been many like patterns. Another such is the notion that a more or less complete decentralization of government is a characteristic necessarily inherent in the Middle Ages; and therefore, if we find a strong monarchy somewhere in the midst of the mediaeval period, that we must not call it mediaeval; it must be an aberration. But because we find that so many of these patterns do not truly fit the existing facts, must we conclude that after all there is nothing whatever whose character warrants us in attaching to it the adjective "mediaeval"? Is there no distinctive mediaeval pattern at all? Or further, is there nothing in our modern culture that we may safely trace back in unbroken continuity into the mediaeval period and term a mediaeval heritage?

In the attempt to list a few things that seem at the same time mediaeval and modern, I shall not venture to touch anything but the field of political institutions and ideas, beyond which my knowledge is mainly but second-hand. And in making even such a tentative list I think we must always bear in mind the vast difference between the earlier and the later part of the long period to which we apply the word "mediaeval." As a whole, I suppose we might roughly describe the epoch generally as one in which rather primitive men gradually and progressively assimilated the more advanced institutions and ideas that antiquity had bequeathed them. It is amazing how long a period of contact is required for men at such a primitive state of culture to make their own the remains of a civilization so much higher than theirs. In western Europe one can hardly make this period of progressive assimilation shorter than seven or eight centuries. It was a long, gradual, progressive development, a slow evolution; and the term "mediaeval" is probably most fittingly applied to the culmination in its later centuries, on Aristotle's general teleological principle that the nature of any developing thing is only fully knowable in the final outcome of that development.

One of the things, probably the most important of all the things in my own particular field, that we seem to owe in largest part to these developments of the Middle Ages, is the institution of limited government, which I take to be the synonym for constitutionalism.

This constitutionalism was, of course, no new thing when the mediaeval records of it first appear. It had been a characteristic of republican Rome, had never been wholly obliterated by the growing absolutism of the Empire, and it was enshrined in the Roman legal sources which the ruder successors of the Romans inherited and gradually came in course of time to assimilate, understand, and apply to their own lives.

More and more I have become impressed lately with the relative importance of this Roman influence upon the mediaeval growth of our own principles of political liberty; an importance that political developments since the Middle Ages have tended to obscure, and one that it has been the usual fashion of the historians of our laws and constitutions to belittle, to ignore, or even to deny. The recent repudiation of Roman law by the Nazis in Germany because it is inconsistent with their totalitarianism makes one wonder if we have not, for a long time, been greatly over-emphasizing the despotic influence of that law in our history, and as seriously under-rating the importance of Roman constitutionalism in the early development of our own.

Dyed-in-the-wool mediaevalists may object to a procedure like this which admits the possibility that events, even of today, may or should affect our interpretation of an epoch as far behind us as the Middle Ages. And yet, as Maitland says, all history is "a seamless web," and the present is a part of it as well as the past. Thus we all admit that the past should influence our ideas and ideals for the present, but if so it is hard to deny the validity of the converse of this: that the outcome of the past in the present should also have some influence upon our estimate of the past, and in fact of the whole drama of human destiny whose final *dénouement* no man can know. In saying this I do not, of course, wish to imply the crude transfer of modern modes of thought and action into past periods, the mechanical undiscriminating discovery of modern factors in the mediaeval world which has constituted probably the chief defect in our histories of the past development of our political institutions and ideas. It is easy enough to find the present in the past if we put the present there in this fashion before we start.

But this slipshod, unscientific method is a far cry from the one I have advocated above, in which we assume the oneness of the entire history of our institutions and insist merely that a careful and discriminating study of their outcome today may be of help toward a fuller understanding of the earlier stages through which this later stage has been reached. To do so in this way, it seems to me, is only to carry out in our historical investigations the sound general principle of Aristotle which I cited a moment ago. The best way to learn most about an acorn is to look at an oak. It is thus, and thus only, that the present should influence our views of the past. But "Art is long and life is fleeting," and if we are to be good mediaevalists we must devote our main attention to the Middle Ages themselves and at the cost of some other periods.

Yet I submit that this must not lead to the narrow view that we should look at nothing else. The true nature of the Middle Ages cannot be fully understood except by some study of their outcome in the Renaissance and of their modern development. We can no more understand the true nature of this period in our history without consideration of its outcome than we could know all about a tadpole without studying the toad. As indicated above, in some things, particularly in the growth of the institutions and ideas with which I have been chiefly concerned, the so-called "Renaissance of the twelfth century" seems to me to be on the whole more significant on a perspective of the whole of history, than the later development to which we usually attach the word "Renaissance." But this is in no way to belittle that later period whose influence is undeniable, and ought to be so to the mediaevalist above all others, because he, more clearly than any others, is able to see the utter falsity of the notion that then for the first time since the ancients men rediscovered both the world and man. He knows that the Renaissance is in many ways only an extension of the Middle Ages, and this knowledge ought to heighten, not to lessen his interest in that later period, even though life is too short to study it in detail; for undoubtedly some of the best and most important elements of the culture of the Renaissance are a heritage from the period before.

It is for considerations like this that I venture to say that the events in Europe even of today or tomorrow, equally with those of the Renaissance, may legitimately influence our interpretation of things as remote as those of the twelfth or the thirteenth century, or even as far back as the seventh or the eighth. If we find, for instance, that the Nazis in Germany are now repudiating Roman Law because the political principles they think it incorporates have proved to be too favorable to individual liberty to suit these promoters of totalitarianism, one is naturally led to ask whether they may not be right in so thinking, and whether we, after all, may not be wrong even in the interpretation of the Middle Ages, in our usual assumption that Roman principles are synonymous with absolutism: that the political essence of this Romanism is the maxim, "Quod principi placuit legis vigorem habet.". . .

In coming, then, at long last, to the subject I am supposed to talk about, the mediaeval in the present, this subject of Roman law furnishes one good example. In England and America at least, we have on the whole been prone to accept without enough examination the thesis that on its political side Roman law in the Middle Ages was but a prop to absolutism. We have usually taken at its face value the assertion of Sir John Fortescue, near the end of the fifteenth century, that the absolutist doctrines contained in such maxims as "quod principi placuit legis vigorem habet," or Ulpian's statement "princeps legibus solutus est" express "the chief principles among the civil laws" ("inter leges civiles praecipua sententia"), as he called them. To one who has accepted this tradition without much question it is something of a shock to look back to the thirteenth century and learn that Bracton sees nothing whatsoever of this kind in Roman law.

Once started on such an investigation, the student soon finds that thirteenth century men generally, unlike those of the fifteenth or the sixteenth, found no absolutism in the law of Rome, but rather constitutionalism. Such absolutist statements as the ones above do not for Bracton express the true central principle either of Roman or of English politics. That central principle is rather to be found in Papinian's dictum "Lex est communis sponsio rei publicae," "the common engagement of the republic," not "the pleasure of the prince." And in this, the mediaeval conception of the political side of Roman law is typical of mediaeval political ideas generally. To men of the thirteenth century Roman political principles and their own seemed essentially alike, not unlike; and neither the Roman nor their own were despotic. In proof of this, other passages of Roman law might easily be cited in addition to the ones we have already noted.

In our own earlier history there is, for example, the famous extract in Edward I's writ of summons to the Parliament of 1295, in which the Archbishop of Canterbury is enjoined, before appearing himself, to secure the presence in person or by deputy of the lower clergy of his province: "Sicut lex justissima, provida circumspectione sacrorum principum stabilita, hortatur et statuit ut quod omnes tangit ab omnibus approbetur, sic et nimis evidenter, ut communis periculis per remedia provisa communiter obvietur." "As a most just law, established by the far-sighted wisdom of sacred princes urges and has ordained that what touches all should be approved by all; equally and most clearly [it implies] that common dangers should be met by remedies provided in common." In its original use, as repeated in Justinian's *Code*, this provision has to do only with the private law, but it is here used as a maxim of state in a matter of the highest political importance. It is true that some have regarded Edward's quotation of it as of very little significance, and Professor G. B. Adams even cites its frequent use in earlier ecclesiastical documents as proof of this; but to me this repeated quotation is an indication not of its unimportance, but rather of the wide prevalence in mediaeval politics of the idea it expresses.

Modern interpretations of this famous

writ have usually failed to notice its emphasis on the inference to be drawn from Justinian's words, as expressed in the added clause "that common dangers should be met by remedies provided in common." This added clause contains the kernel of the writ, and indicates the royal purpose in calling up the extraordinary number of the lower clergy. The writ is, in fact, Edward's anticipation of and answer to the principle of the papal bull *Clericis laicos* of the next year; and it is precisely the same answer, though much more politely worded, as that of Philip the Fair, expressed in the well-known document printed by Depuy, beginning with the words *Antequam essent clerici*. It was very natural and very effective, in a writ summoning the clergy to an assembly in which a large grant was to be asked for, thus to cite in justification a maxim which the clergy themselves had used so long and so often in their own provincial assemblies. The political idea underlying this maxim finds constant expression, not only in the words of the thirteenth century, in England, in France, and in many other parts of western Europe; but in the institutions as well.

It is to such institutions that I should like in the next place to turn as a further example of the mediaeval in its influence upon the modern. It is a commonplace of modern constitutional history that the power of the purse has been the principal means of securing and maintaining the liberties of the subject against the encroachments of the prince. Probably in no part of our constitutional history is the influence of the Middle Ages upon the modern world more obvious than here. For the constitutional principle just mentioned can be shown to be the outgrowth, the gradual and at times almost unperceived outgrowth, of the mediaeval principle that a feudal lord in most cases can exact no aid from his vassal save with the consent of all like vassals of the same fief. The whole principle contained in our maxim, "no taxation without representation," has this feudal practice as its origin.

This is probably so obvious and so generally admitted that it needs little proof or illustration. But one aspect of it we are likely to overlook. These rights of the vassal are proprietary rights, and we are likely to give them a definition as narrow as our own modern definition of proprietary rights. This, however, is to misinterpret the nature of these limitations and vastly to lessen the importance of the principle of consent in the Middle Ages. For these rights of vassals, though protected by what we should call the land-law, included almost all of those rights which today we term "personal," such as the right to office, the right to immunities, or, as they were usually called then, to "liberties" or franchises, and even to the right to one's security in his social and personal status. A serf, for example, was protected against the abuse by his lord of rights which we call "personal" by remedies which it is difficult to distinguish from those used for the protection of the seisin of land. One might be truly said to have been "seized" of the rights securing his person as much as of those protecting his fief. It may be said of the Middle Ages generally, then, that private rights were immune from governmental encroachment under the political principles of the time. In this the Middle Ages shared the principles of Roman Law, and no doubt it was this common feature of both systems that enabled Glanvil and Bracton and all the jurists in the period between to liken the English Law in so many respects to the Roman.

If we are estimating the importance of the mediaeval in the modern in this field from which I have chosen to illustrate it, this constitutionalism, this limitation of governmental authority by private right, is the main tradition handed down by the Middle Ages to the modern world. It is the chief element in the political part of our mediaeval heritage. With the decay of feudal institutions, however, the sanctions by which these principles were maintained in practice tended to be greatly weakened, and no doubt it is the lawlessness of this later period of weakness following the decay of the feudal and preceding the development of the national sanctions for law, which has led to the popular impression that the Middle Ages as a whole are nothing more than one long stretch of uncontrolled violence. No doubt the violence of this later period may also be considered to be the chief cause of the increasing power of monarchy and the almost unlimited theories of obedience which we find among the chief characteristics of the period of the Renaissance. As was said then, it is better to submit to one tyrant than to a thousand. And without doubt the weakness of these sanctions of law in the later Middle Ages is a prime cause of the strength of monarchy in the period immediately following. In the reaction and revolution which in time were provoked in the period of the Renaissance or afterward by the extension and abuse of these powers of government we may find the true causes of the modern sanctions for the subjects' rights. In the early stages at least of this revolution the precedents cited in favor of liberty are largely drawn from the Middle Ages.

The particular side of the Middle Ages with which we have been dealing certainly offers little proof of either of the extreme interpretations that we find in modern times. It was both a lawful and a lawless period. At no time was law more insisted upon, but at times few of these laws were observed. When we consider this period in comparison with periods following, the same discrimination is necessary. The political theory of that time included more limitations upon governmental power than many theories of a much later time. It may indeed be said that political absolutism, at least as a theory of government, is a modern and not a mediaeval notion. In fact, the great champions of liberty against oppression, if their own words are to be trusted, have fought for the maintenance of liberties inherited from the Middle Ages. In our own day such traditional conceptions of liberty appear less seldom perhaps, for many liberals, and certainly most extreme radicals, are now frequently struggling for rights for which the Middle Ages can furnish few precedents. But this should not blind us to the all-important fact that for a long period in this historic struggle; indeed for the whole of the early part of it, it was for their mediaeval inheritance that all opponents of oppression engaged.

The lesson of it all is discrimination. If some modern elements had not been added to our mediaeval inheritance, elements non-existent before modern times, even that inheritance could scarcely have persisted; and yet the central principle for which free men have always fought, the sanctity of law against oppressive will, is a principle recognized by our mediaeval ancestors as fully as by ourselves, and more fully, apparently, than by their successors of the sixteenth century. We cannot, therefore, truly entertain notions of the Middle Ages which make it one long, dreary epoch of stagnation, of insecurity, of lawless violence; neither can we truly consider it the Golden Age that some have pictured. What we need above all is discrimination and yet more discrimination.

TOWARD A MORE POSITIVE EVALUATION OF THE FIFTEENTH-CENTURY RENAISSANCE: *Part I*

HANS BARON

Dr. Hans Baron, born and educated in Germany, is now associated with the Newberry Library in Chicago. A very productive scholar, Dr. Baron has studied the civilization of the Renaissance intensively, especially that of Florence. His writings center on the relation and interconnection between ideas and the political and social structure of the civilization of Renaissance Italy. The following discussion of its political aspects is part of a paper given by Dr. Baron at a session of the 1941 convention of the American Historical Association which was devoted to the problem of the Renaissance. The balance of this paper which relates to science is given in a subsequent selection.

THE tendency to minimize the role played by fifteenth-century Italy in the emergence of the modern world is by no means the product of conditions peculiar to the field of science. In political history, when attention is focussed on such elements of the modern state as constitutionally guaranteed civil rights and parliamentary representation on a nation-wide basis, it is difficult to avoid similar negative conclusions about the contribution made by the Renaissance. Bearing in mind such aspects of the modern state, Professor McIlwain in a suggestive lecture before the Mediaeval Academy recently gave it as his opinion that "what Professor Haskins has termed 'the Renaissance of the twelfth century' marks a more fundamental change" and "seems to be on the whole more significant in a perspective of the whole history, than the later development to which we usually attach the word 'Renaissance.'" Opinions like these, more or less pronounced, are probably held by the majority of present-day historians of English law. They form, for instance, the key-note of R. W. and A. J. Carlyle's six volumes on *Mediaeval Political Theory in the West*. Again, students who place greater emphasis on the growth of administration and on the rise of a trained, nationally-minded bureaucracy frequently trace the pedigree of the modern state from Norman institutions or from the Sicilian monarchy of Frederick II to the jurist-administration of fourteenth-century France, and then to the centralized organization of the absolute monarchy of the seventeenth and eighteenth centuries — without having recourse to any essential contributions derived from the Renaissance.

Yet in the field of political history one can hardly say that this new balance has been established beyond doubt. No sooner are attempts made to reverse what is regarded as an over-emphasis on the Renaissance, than some one comes forward to

From Hans Baron, "Toward a More Positive Evaluation of the Fifteenth-Century Renaissance," in the *Journal of the History of Ideas*, IV (1943), 22–27. By permission of the editors of the *Journal of the History of Ideas*.

enhance old claims for some priority of fifteenth-century Italy. The way in which discussions have developed in the present meeting reflects this situation. In a vein very different from that of Dr. Durand's criticism of the *"primato dell'Italia* in the field of science," Professor Nelson's contribution from political history has been a vigorous restatement of the thesis — which was virtually that of Ranke — that the state-system of the fifteenth-century Italy, composed of Venice, Milan, Florence, Naples, and the Papal State, witnessed the origin of modern balance-of-power diplomacy. In other words, the differences of opinion that embarrass us in our assessment of the Renaissance cut across the border-line between political and intellectual history. In every field of study we are faced with the same problem. In cases without number we learned to look at modern ideas and institutions as an outgrowth of medieval conditions, which have revealed themselves as indispensable stages in the historical continuity. But at the same time students ask: does this view, however undisputed it may be, force us henceforth to disclaim all that was once deemed the "modern" face and the "precursorship" of the Italian Renaissance? Apparently there are two sides to the picture. In order to understand their complementary truth, a brief methodological digression seems advisable.

When Burckhardt coined the famous phrase that the Italian of the Renaissance was "the first-born among the sons of modern Europe," he certainly was prompted by what we must today call an over-estimate of the direct impact of the Italian Renaissance on the rise of the modern world. He underrated the continuity of medieval conditions in thought, in politics, and in many spheres of life. On the other hand, by the phrase "first-born son of modern Europe" he did not mean simply that the ideas and institutions of the modern world must be traced largely to fourteenth- and fifteenth-century Italy as their historical source. If the words are taken literally, the meaning is that fifteenth-century Italy saw

the coming of the first member of a family that subsequently spread throughout the western world — the first specimen of a new species. Burckhardt was thinking of a pattern of society, education, and thought kindred in its sociological and cultural structure to the life of the later West, and therefore potentially stimulating to all subsequent generations — the *prototype* far more than the *origin* of the modern world.

The label of "historical significance" we so frequently employ is in fact made to cover two essentially different types of relationship between the past and the present. On the one hand, in our evaluation of past periods we view history as if it were a chain, in which the role of each link is merely to bridge the gap between the preceding and following links. But were this the only basis of historical evaluation, our estimate of the import of ancient Greece and Rome for the modern world would be much lower than it is. As a matter of fact, we constantly make use of a second method of historical evaluation, one based on the realization that history is more than a mere chain in which each link has contacts only with its neighbors. For instance, the political and ethical ideals of the Greek city-state may become powerless in the Hellenistic period immediately following, but be revived to historical potency whenever kindred patterns of life emerge — as in Cicero's Rome, in the fifteenth century, in Bacon's England, and possibly in our own day, or in days to come. Ideas of God, the world, space and time, conceived in a religious atmosphere, may later affect the whole fabric of culture and of thought, when kindred thought-patterns become possible in the sphere of science.

These are no doubt truisms. Yet they are easily overlooked. What they imply is that in every given case our attention must be turned both to the rôle of a period as a link in the chain of continuity, and to its potential affinities, in intellectual and social structure, to later periods. This balance of historical emphasis, I think, has recently been neglected in our study of the Renaissance.

When it is taken into account, the present antagonism between two apparently irreconcilable schools of thought in the appraisal of the fifteenth century is largely explained.

In the field of political history it is comparatively easy to discern both the merits and the limitations of the two methods. From the outset it is improbable that representative government and a centralized administration — institutions made to answer the specific problems of large nation-states — could have been substantially promoted by the conditions in the small city-republics and tyrannies of fifteenth-century Italy. There is no doubt that the medieval assembly of the crown vassals, giving counsel to their king, and the emergence of a new *noblesse de robe* in the national monarchies, were the chief, if not the only, roots of parliamentarism and bureaucracy in England and France. Yet this verdict passed from the perspective of the nation-state leaves unsolved all the questions which might reveal a *structural* kinship of fifteenth-century Italy with those patterns of political and social life which eventually emerged in the modern West.

In the case of the English constitution, increasing knowledge of its preparation throughout the Middle Ages has not removed the gap between "medieval constitutionalism" and "modern constitutionalism." In spite of the importance attached by Professor McIlwain to the institutions and thought of the twelfth and thirteenth centuries, no one has emphasized more strongly than he himself that to find in fifteenth-century England any ideas of republican participation by the people in the government or of active control of the administration by the nation, is to read modern concepts into the medieval context. If it is true that parliamentary institutions and the limitation of despotic monarchy were growing in feudal Europe from the twelfth century onward, it is also true that "medieval constitutionalism," meaning subordination of the king to the law and the imposition of restrictions upon him in matters of

jurisdiction, was one thing, while the modern idea "that the members of a free state must be true citizens" by having "a part in its control" (as Professor McIlwain puts it) is another. The latter — modern — notion, which had had its major precedent in the ancient world, played no role in England until the middle of the seventeenth century, i.e., after the cataclysm of the Civil War.

Yet in the smaller orbit of the Italian city-state the basic features of modern government by discussion and participation of the citizens in political control appeared as early as the twelfth century. In this milieu, ideas of citizenship that were destined to become, in McIlwain's words, "the commonplace of all political thought in modern times" came to the fore at once when political thought of the Scholastics was transplanted into the urban atmosphere. The fact that these ideas survived throughout the Quattrocento is fundamental for the appraisal of its political and intellectual make-up. Republican freedom and civic initiative, continuing through the "Age of the Despots," were forced to develop their full bearing on political ideals and thought in their life-or-death struggle with Renaissance tyranny. It is because of this survival of civic initiative in geographic proximity to bureaucratic-unifying absolutism that the whole range of modern political experience was traversed in the fifteenth century, and this so rapidly that by the end of the century many of the basic tenets of modern political science had matured, and been set forth in works of European scope by Machiavelli and Guicciardini.

Now Professor Nelson has recalled one of the most significant implications of these conditions, namely, that by the second half of the fifteenth century integration and interplay of the Italian states had reached a point where they produced something like a prelude to the later European power-system. One may go further and conclude that there must have been an underlying general affinity between the texture of political life in Renaissance Italy and the structure of the modern state. To refer to one example of recent date, when Professor Heckscher, in his broad study of modern Mercantilism, confronted the medieval and modern economic pattern by pointing out the interrelationship between industrial "Protectionism" and the modern state, he found the first appearance of the protectionist policy of the modern type in the Italian city-states and even more in the urbanized regional states which formed the power-system of fifteenth-century Italy. From my own knowledge I should say that it is possible to round out such analogies for the whole orbit of political life. For instance, not only was the mechanism of modern power-diplomacy anticipated in the time of Lorenzo de' Medici . . . , but the idea of a "balance" between equal members of a state-system then, as later in the modern West, issued from a cycle of events that had started with the threat by one power to transform the whole system into a single universal state — a threat followed by wars of independence, from which the individual states emerged conscious of their identity, strengthened in national feeling, with the will to assert themselves in a balance of power. In short, it is not alone in diplomatic technique (the feature which immediately spread from Italy throughout Europe), but in the inherent dynamics of international relations that Renaissance Italy foreshadowed the character of the family of modern western nations.

Bearing these facts in mind, we shall find it hard to subscribe to any judgment to the effect that, from the viewpoint of political ideas and conditions, the twelfth century was more significant than the fifteenth century. At the present stage of our knowledge, the only fair judgment seems to be one not couched in the terms of an alternative. As far as the political pattern of modern life is characterized by the existence of nation-states, spanning a large geographical area by virtue of representative government, the foundation laid in the Middle Ages looms larger indeed than any possible contribution by the Italian Renaissance. Still, when we ask what after all distinguishes modern political life from the feudal epoch, it is of equal significance that the *state of aggregation* of the modern world, as it were, was first foreshadowed in the Italian Renaissance, with a political system of smaller compass and simpler sociological conditions — albeit the nation-state and the representative system had not yet entered into the historical compound.

SOCIOLOGY OF THE RENAISSANCE

ALFRED VON MARTIN

Alfred von Martin, born in 1882, has taught at the universities of Göttingen and Munich. His many books, dealing with sociological interpretations of the medieval, Renaissance, and modern scenes, are widely known. His book on the religion of Burckhardt was confiscated by the Gestapo in 1942.

INTRODUCTION

Inertia and motion, static and dynamic are fundamental categories with which to begin a sociological approach to history. It must be said, though, that history knows inertia in a relative sense only: the decisive question is whether inertia or change predominates.

The centre of gravity of mediaeval society was the land, was the soil. With the Renaissance the economic and thus the social emphasis moves into the town: from the conservative to the liberal, for the town is a changeable and changing element. Mediaeval society was founded upon a static order of Estates, sanctioned by the Church. Everyone was assigned to his place by nature, i.e. by God himself, and any attempt to break away from it was a revolt against the divine order. Everyone was confined within strictly defined limits, which were imposed and enforced by the ruling Estates, the clergy and the feudal nobility. The King himself was bound to rule according to definite laws: he had to carry out his reciprocal obligations towards his vassals; he had to treat the Church according to the principles of *justitia*. Otherwise his vassals had a right of rebellion, and the Church denounced him who had strayed from his assigned position as a *tryrannus*. The burgher could be fitted into this order by the Church so long as he remained the modest middle-class man, who saw himself as a part of the established order, living in the mediaeval town which was still based upon a primary economy and a conservative scheme of things. Even in Renaissance Italy this *petite bourgeoisie* had its outlook closely circumscribed by such an order of society. But, as the burghers became a power with the rise of a money economy, as the small artisan became the great merchant, we find a gradual emancipation from the traditional forms of society and the mediaeval outlook: there was a revolt against those sections of society which were most dependent upon this structure and upon these ways of thought, by virtue of which they exercised their authority. We find arising against the privileged clergy and the feudal nobility the bourgeoisie, which was throwing off their tutelage and emerging on the twin props of money and intellect as a bourgeoisie of "liberal" character. By revolting against the old domination they also freed themselves from the old community ties which had been interlinked with it. Blood, tradition and group feeling had been the basis of the community relationships as well as of the old domination. The democratic and urban spirit was destroying the old social forms and the "natural" and accepted divine order. It thus be-

From *Sociology of the Renaissance*, translated for the *International Library of Sociology and Social Reconstruction* from *Soziologie der Renaissance* (Stuttgart, 1932), pp. 1–19. By permission of the Oxford University Press and Routledge and Kegan Paul Ltd. Copyright 1944.

came necessary to order the world starting from the individual and to shape it, as it were, like a work of art. The guiding rules in this task accorded with those liberal aims set by the constructive will of the bourgeoisie.

Life in a primary community is apt to produce a conservative type of thought, a religious way of thought which orders the world in an authoritarian manner. Everything temporal is to it no more than a parable, a symbol of the metaphysical, and nature is but a reflection of the transcendental. But the bourgeois world as seen from the coolly calculating, realist point of view of the city state is a world that has lost its magic. The liberal mode of thought of the emancipated individual attempts to control the outside world more and more consciously. Thus community becomes society, and thus arises the new domination by a new oligarchy, the capitalist domination by the moneyed great bourgeoisie, which exploits those "democratic" tendencies which had destroyed feudalism, as the best way to ensure its own domination. In the Middle Ages political power with religious sanction had prevailed: now comes the era of an intellectually supported economic power. Religion as well as politics becomes a means, just as previously commerce and secular culture had been no more than the means to an end.

The Middle Ages in their social structure as well as in their thought had a rigidly graduated system. There was a pyramid of Estates as well as a pyramid of values. Now these pyramids are about to be destroyed, and "free competition" is proclaimed as the law of nature. God and blood, the traditional powers, are deposed, and though they maintain some of their importance their dominance is shattered.

The spirit of capitalism which begins to rule the modern world with the Renaissance deprives the world of the divine element in order to make it more real. But the spirit of early capitalism did not as yet dehumanize it. Reason was not as yet rated above humanity; it was not yet the be-all

and end-all of all action. Riches were, as yet, no more than a means to independence, respect and fame (L. B. Alberti). Although time was beginning to become scarce, the individual could yet lead a cultured existence and see himself as a full personality. The culture of Renaissance Italy, and only Italy knew a genuine Renaissance, contained from the very beginning certain aristocratic elements and tended to emphasize them increasingly. It is significant that Italy led the way in the development of early, but by no means of full capitalism.

Thus the typological importance of the Renaissance is that it marks the first cultural and social breach between the Middle Ages and modern times: it is a typical early stage of the modern age. And the outstanding ideal type is the Italian situation above all in Florence. Jakob Burckhardt could already write: "The Florentine was the model and prototype of the present-day Italian and of the modern European in general," and Pöhlmann said that we find in Florence "the most varied expression of the spirit of modern times to be seen anywhere at the end of the Middle Ages or within so confined an area." The reasons for this advanced position of Italy, and above all of Florence, are to be found in political, constitutional, economic, social and educational history, as well as in the relations with the Church.

But for the sociologist the interest of the period lies in the fact that it presents him with a complete rhythmic progression of the ideal type of a cultural epoch dominated by the bourgeoisie. The differentiation of Early, Full and Late Renaissance, originally devised by the art critic, finds its sociological meaning in those social changes which are expressed in the stylistic ones. The prelude to the bourgeois era which we call the Renaissance begins in the spirit of democracy and ends in the spirit of the court. The first phase represents the rise of a few above the rest. This is followed by the securing of their newly won exalted position and the attempt to establish relations with the feudal aristocracy and to adopt their way of life. From the very beginning, that part of the bourgeoisie which gave its character to the period, i.e. the capitalist entrepreneurs, feels itself called upon to rule. In order to achieve this end it must first eliminate the former rulers on its "Right" by making an alliance with the "Left." But from the very beginning it has a tendency toward the "Right"; a tendency to intermix with the traditional ruling classes, to adopt their way of life, their attitude and their mode of thought and to attempt to become part of feudal "good" society.

The humanists — representatives of the intelligentsia — follow the same road and feel themselves tied to the new elite; whether this attachment was voluntary or not is of secondary importance here. Under the circumstances "democracy" meant no more than opposition to the privileges of the old powers, the clergy and the feudal nobility; hence the negation of those values which served to uphold their special position; it meant a new, bourgeois principle of selection according to purely individual criteria and not according to birth and rank. But liberty was not made into a revolutionary principle symbolizing an onslaught upon all and every established authority. In particular the Church was respected as an authoritative institution, and the only aim of the bourgeoisie was to vindicate its right to a position of importance. "A complete self-disarmament, such as the upper Estates carried through before the Revolution in France under the influence of Rousseau, was out of the question among these utilitarian Italians" (F. G. J. von Bezold). This bourgeoisie of the Renaissance had a strong sense of what would enhance its power; its rationalism served it without ever endangering its position.

THE NEW DYNAMIC

Changes in Social Structure

"Italy, always delighting in a new thing, has lost all stability . . . ; a servant may easily become a king." It was the new power of money that made Aeneas Sylvius say this, a power which changes and sets in motion. For it is a part of the "power of money to subject all walks of life to its tempo" (Simmel). In an era of primary economy the individual was immediately dependent upon the group and the interchange of services linked him closely to the community; but now money makes the individual independent because, unlike the soil, it gives mobility. "Cash payments" are now "the tie between people" (Lujo Brentano); the relationship between employer and employed is based upon a free contract, with each party to it determined to secure the utmost advantage. At the stage of development represented by a primary economy human and personal relationships predominated; a money economy makes all these relationships more objective.

Authority and tradition were able to dominate the mediaeval economy because of the methods of the self-sufficient, individual undertaking; but the resulting limitations become unbearable when the economic system of segregated small or medium-sized units is replaced by capitalist enterprises pointing the way to the factory system, and when industry begins to produce for a larger market, the world market in fact.

Now competition becomes a serious factor, whereas the essence of the guild organization, with its price fixing and compulsory corporization, had been the elimination of competition. In those days the individual had been unfree but secure — as in a family. But for obvious reasons, that had been possible only in an economy designed to satisfy immediate and local needs. Even the professional trader had been able to maintain the characteristics of the artisan owing to his unchanging methods and life. As long as the horizon remained comparatively limited all this was possible, but as soon as the horizon expands, as great money fortunes are accumulated (in the Middle Ages fortunes consisted solely of land), these conditions are bound to disappear. The great merchants and moneyed men regard the rules of the guild as so many fetters, and they know how to rid themselves of them. In Florence they free themselves from the restrictions of the guilds and achieve individual freedom to carry on trade and commerce, thus freeing themselves from all the mediaeval barriers against the rise of a class of real entrepreneurs. The individualist spirit of early capitalism thus replaces the corporate spirit of the mediaeval burgher.

The Florentine development was both typical and the first in point of time. The townspeople of the Middle Ages were "essentially similar and economically independent individuals" (Doren); all this was fundamentally altered by the increasing power of mobile capital. In step with the industrial developments we find radical alterations in the social structure, for now an elite of capitalists was forming itself; it no longer took part in manual work, but was active in the sphere of organization and management, standing apart from the remainder of the middle class and the working proletariat. The wage-earners — excluded from the possession of the means of production and from all political rights — were ruthlessly exploited and even deprived of the right of association. But the mercantile and industrial capitalist elements also asserted their power over the master craftsmen, the *popolo grasso* of the *arti maggiori* over the *popolo minuto* of the *arti minori*. And it was the great merchants, leading the *arti maggiori*, who in 1293 made the guild organization into the basis of the Florentine constitution. Only formally speaking was this a victory of a broad middle-class democracy (cf. Davidson). Not the "people," but the monetary power of the upper guilds defeated the feudal aristocracy, and the middle class represented by the lower guilds was for all intents and purposes excluded from power. The Florentine constitution of 1293 gave power to a selected plutocracy. The "rule of the people" remained an ideological façade, a slogan for the masses. It was designed to tie them to the new rulers, and deck out as the rule of justice the new form of government which degraded and deprived of political rights the whole feudal class. The struggle against the feudal aristocracy was the first trial of strength of the *haute bourgeoisie*, in which it needed the support of the middle and small bourgeoisie.

It is true to say that feudalism had never been fully established in Italy, yet even Florence had a mediaeval constitution which had to be destroyed. Eberhard Gothein, in his *Renaissance in Süditalien*, shows to how small an extent the legislation even of a Frederick II had destroyed feudalism in southern Italy, and how it was systematically re-established in Renaissance Naples. But on the other hand, he also shows how largely it had become "an empty form, a lie" even there; how much a "fiction" and a "disguise" which no longer corresponded to reality. "The spirit of ruler and ruled alike had long since outgrown the ideas of feudalism"; "these forms of tenure, deprived of their pristine meaning," had become fictitious. The primacy of the old rulers had corresponded to their military importance, the importance of the heavy cavalry of the vassal and his followers. In the measure in which the infantry, the weapon of the burghers, acquired increasing and then overwhelming tactical importance, the nobility was bound to take a place of secondary rank even in its very own military sphere. But the same was true of economic and cultural trends: the nobility was no longer at home in an era of reason. Even though the nobility had — before the bourgeois — fought against the Church as the sole arbiter of conscience, it was now deprived of the basis of its power — the monopoly in military matters and the link of wealth with landed property. It stood, senile and outlived, in the midst of a new era. Even its respect for "honour" was anachronistic; one remembers Vespasiano da Bisticci's story of King Alfonso's impulsive refusal to destroy the Genoese fleet by purely technical means, because it seemed unchivalrous to do so. Such scruples were bound to appear as old-fashioned, aristocratic prejudices to an era which rationally shaped its means to serve its ends, and reckoned only the chances of success. Against an ideology which bases its power upon an empty legitimacy, which is therefore felt to be false, against such an ideology the realistic bourgeois stakes the reality of power, for it alone impresses him, whereas its absence appears contemptible. But the basis of power in a money economy is twofold: (a) the possession of money and (b) an orderly management of business. Giovanni Villani believes that the disorderly management of their resources by the (Teutonic) feudal nobility forced them to satisfy their need for money by arbitrary means such as violence and faithlessness. It is part of the self-respect of the great bourgeois that he, a good merchant, has no need of such methods, for economic reason gives him a way of calculating correctly; it is here that he sees the superiority of his civilization, the civilization of the towns.

The mediaeval system knew in the field of economics only one type of order, the order of the small men, peasants and artisans, who by the work of their hands earned their keep, in accordance with the necessities of their rank, their traditionally fixed "needs." Apart from this static order, which applied to the vast majority, there was the static disorder in which the great lords, the rich of pre-capitalist days, led their particular lives. It did not matter whether they were secular magnates or among those priests who, according to Alberti, desired to outdo all in splendour and display, in inclination to inactivity and the absence of all economy. As a matter of fact, such an unregulated and indolent mode of life led to the economic ruin of the majority of the old noble families. In contradistinction to the nobleman as well as the mediaeval peasant or artisan, the bourgeois entrepreneur calculates; he thinks rationally, not traditionally; he does not desire the static (i.e. he does not acquiesce in the customary and the traditional) or the disorderly but the dynamic (i.e. he is impelled towards something new) and the orderly.

He calculates, and his calculations take the long-term view. All sentiment (such as the peasant's love for his own or the pride that the artisan takes in his handiwork) is foreign to him. What he values is the drive and discipline of work, directed singlemindedly toward an end. It is this that produces order as a human work of art.

But characteristic of the Renaissance is a far-reaching assimilation of the nobility to the new conditions and the reception of the nobles in the towns. The country nobility, in so far as it is not destroyed by "chivalrous feuds and extravagance, settles in the town" and takes up commercial activities. It thus wins for itself wealth, and upon that basis a new political power; in the process it becomes bourgeois in its nature, attitude and modes of thought, so that the bourgeois is no longer determined by his ancestry. This type of noble intermarries with the great patrician families and together with them forms an exclusive aristocracy of commerce. This process is accelerated by the inclination of those families which are not noble to invest their industrial and commercial profits in land. This is done in the interest of the prestige of their firm and their own social standing, perhaps after they have ruined the original noble owners. It leads to a complete reconstitution of "good society"; it is a new aristocracy of talent and determination (in place of birth and rank), which begins by combining economic with political prowess, but whose mode of life is on the whole determined by the economic, i.e. the bourgeois, element.

The New Individualist Entrepreneur

In acquiring power and social standing through wealth, the financially powerful bourgeoisie had thus become superior to the nobility, even in politics. What was fundamentally new was the rational management of money and the investment of capital. Capital had a creative effect and put a premium on ingenuity and enterprise. In the Middle Ages, a period of predominantly agricultural production, interest had centred upon consumption; after all, it is relatively impossible either to lose or increase landed property, which is essentially static. Only money, in the form of productive capital, creates the unlimited openings which emphasize the problem of acquisition as against that of consumption. With this growth in scope came the desire to exploit it: the enlargement of business increased the will and the ability to overcome the problems involved. The stability of an as yet static economy was upset by a dynamic element which increasingly and fundamentally altered its whole character. A progressive and expansive force was inherent in the new type of economic man and the new economy, a force which was to break up slowly but surely the old world of small economic unit. Thus an economy of money and credit made possible the hitherto unknown spirit of enterprise in economic matters.

It became possible in quite a new sense to follow "enterprising" aims since they could be pursued by completely rational means, by the full exploitation of the possibilities inherent in a money economy. The rationally calculating foresight of the merchant served to fashion in addition to the art of trade also the arts of statecraft and of war. The bourgeois, having gained his position of power, continued to press on and, in accordance with his psychology and will to power, appeared as a freely competing capitalist entrepreneur not only in commerce but also in political matters. It might be that he combined the functions of business magnate and political leader (as did the Medici, who relied upon their wealth and their position as party leaders), or he might, by capitalist methods, secure free disposal over a military force as a *condottiere* or over a subdued state as *nuovo principe.*

It is one of the traits of the early capitalist civilization of the Renaissance that business and politics became so thoroughly interdependent that it is impossible to separate the interests that they represented. We can see this clearly already in the case of Giovanni Villani. Business methods served political ends, political means served economic ends. Political and economic credit were already inseparable. The fame and glory of a state (also increased by successful wars) were reflected in profits. On the other hand, we can already discern the difficulties brought about by the cosmopolitan character of the new power of money and the interlocking of international capital. Nevertheless, this obstacle to vigorous foreign policies was more than offset by the stimulus it gave to imperialist aims. The numerically small group of commercial and industrial magnates which at home had won political along with economic power, pursued in its external relations, too, a policy fashioned on broad lines — a policy of territorial expansion (such as the Florentine conquest of the ports of Pisa and Livorno, which was to benefit Florentine seaborne trade) or of winning new markets which was pursued "even at the price of internal unrest and without hesitating to conjure up war and its misery" (Doren). This may be contrasted with the more restricted policy of the *petit bourgeois,* the artisan, whose goal was a "bourgeois" existence and the "peaceful comfort of a small circle" (Doren). The entrepreneur, abroad as at home, was turning the state to his own ends.

But above all, the state itself was now becoming a capitalist entrepreneur; the politician began to calculate and politics were becoming rational. Political decisions were influenced by commercial motives, and politics were closely circumscribed by the categories of means and ends dictated by bourgeois aims and interests. We see politics pervaded by the spirit of reason, which had been alien to the mediaeval state at a time when the Church had been the one rationally guided institution. It is of minor importance whether the bourgeoisie democratically controlled the state or whether the bourgeois methods were adopted by an absolutist state in the shape of mercantilism and rational statecraft. In both cases realistic policy guided by economic considerations provided the contrast, typical of the age, with the practices of the Middle Ages, which had been sustained by the privileged Estates, the clergy and the feudal nobility. The attack upon these classes reveals a complete parallelism between the legislation of the first modern absolutist state, the realm of Frederick II in Lower Italy, and the Florentine *Ordinamenti della Giustizia,* where justice means, in a completely modern sense, the abolition of traditional privileges. In this way the modern monarchy and the formal democracy of a city-state fulfilled the same function: both were adequate to deal with the new social reality created by economic developments. These forms of government represented the two possible ways of adjusting the nature of the state to the nature of society. Accordingly, the Italian despotisms or *Signorie* continued along lines laid down by the town commune: both were built upon the foundation of the new money economy, the free development of individual forces and, on the other hand, the centralization of all power which increasingly substituted administrative for constitutional principles and subjected all spheres of life to conscious and rational regulation. The unifying factor was no longer an organic and communal one (e.g. blood relationship, neighbourhood or the relationships of service) but an artificial and mechanized social organization which cut adrift even from the old religious and moral power and proclaimed the *ratio status* as an expression of the secular nature of a state which was its own law. The resulting statecraft was "objective" and without prejudices, guided only by the needs of the situation and the desired end and consisting only of a pure calculation of power relationships. It was an entirely methodicized, objective and soulless craft and the system of a science and technique of state management.

The Norman state of Roger II showed already, at a very early date, the tendency towards bourgeois valuations, i.e. a spirit of sober calculation and the prominence given to ability and efficiency rather than to birth and rank. At the time of Roger's death Georgio Majo, the son of a Bari merchant who made big deals in oil, was High Chancellor of the Sicilian kingdom. Roger himself had already built up a professional civil service and sponsored a conscious economic policy (cf. his foundation of industries). Using these foundations, Frederick II loosened the old ties by limiting the rights of the Church and the feudal nobility in favour of a centralized organization which used fiscal and rational methods and employed a salaried bureaucracy and an army of mercenaries. Even the modern trait of basic distrust, of not trusting one's fellowmen — that characteristic of society as opposed to the community, which means traditional trust or confidence — which we later find in the urban communes, already characterized the regime of Frederick II: "the whole machinery of administration was so constructed that one section of it watched and controlled the others as much as was possible" (Ed. Winkelmann). And the enlightened despot knew how to exploit the magic position assigned to the mediaeval emperors as providing a prop for his rule and serving as an ideology to counter the papal theory of the two swords.

This Norman kingdom was in need of a rational basis in legislation and administration because it was a state built upon the might of the sword and the powerful personality (E. Caspar). It was for this reason that Burckhardt earlier pointed out its similarity to the *condottiere* states of the Quattrocento. These were "purely factual" structures relying on talent and virtuosity to assure their survival. In such an artificially created situation "only high personal ability" and carefully calculated conduct could master the perpetual menaces. In these states which lacked any traditional sanction the conception of the state as a task for conscious construction had to develop. And thus all depended upon the objective and correct attack upon this task by the proper constructor: to support this new objectivity the modern individual appeared. There was no distinction between the prince and the state: its power was his power, its weakness was his weakness. Therefore the "tyrant," himself the negation of the static mediaeval ideal of the *rex iustus*, has to be judged by the historical and political criterion of "greatness" disregarding the criteria of morals and religion.

The prototype of the combination of the "spirit of enterprise" and the "bourgeois spirit," the two elements that Sombart distinguishes in the capitalist spirit, was the combination of war and business. We find it, even before the Crusades, in the Italian ports. "The warlike enterprises of the Italian sea-trading towns" — Pisa, Genoa, Venice — often "had the character of shareholding ventures," the share in the loot being distributed according to the extent of participation and whether it was only in the capacity of soldier or by the provision of capital (Lujo Brentano). And as a military profession at the disposal of the highest bidder developed, war became increasingly a matter of big business for the military entrepreneur, the *condottiere,* who "with the shrewd sense of a modern speculator changed sides and even fixed in advance the price of an expected victory" (v. Bezold), as well as for his employer. Stefano Porcaro debated before the Signoria at Florence whether it be "more profitable" to fight one's battles with a levy of citizens or with mercenaries, and he concluded that, in spite of the cost, it was "safer and more useful" to settle the business with money.

The Curia itself had to bow to the new trends which made for clearly circumscribed sovereignties forming the basis of financial power. The Vatican "was increasingly robbed of its economic basis in the shape of the powers of taxation of the Church Universal; after the Great Schism it had to create its own state as a necessary foundation" (Clemens Bauer): thus its monetary needs involved it in the internal Italian struggles.

New Modes of Thought

The new mode of thought, evident in all these developments, naturally emanated from an upper class only. The middle class *petit bourgeois,* whose attitude we see in Vespasiano da Bisticci, remained essentially conservative. He still clung to a patriarchal order divided into estates of a static nature. He regarded as "just" the existing state of affairs, with which one should moreover remain content. Honest and straightforward, he took the view of a "good Christian and a good citizen." His simple piety knew no problems; he defended his faith as an absolute truth against the modern, liberal and intellectual belief that everything may be subjected to discussion: he was indignant with the "many unbelievers" who "dispute about the immortality of the soul as though it were a matter for discussion," seeing that it was "almost madness to cast doubt on so great a matter in the face of the testimony of so many eminent men." Here we see a way of thought that was traditional and tied to authority; there is in it no individualist emancipation, so much so, in fact, that Vespasiano could regard a name as a "matter of indifference." And yet this middle class was easily impressed and it bestowed its admiration where it could not really follow. It had to pay tribute to what impressed it and thus admitted, despite itself, valuations which ran counter to its own. Of course, it demanded that glory be not immorally acquired, but it also realized that the great *"quegli che governano gli stati e che vogliono essere innanzi agli altri,"* are not always able to keep to the rules of morality. And the Church itself at once came to the rescue! What, after all, was the purpose of indulgences? Infringements of the moral code could be expiated in money. So even the middle class made money the last instance, thanks to the lead given by the Church. On the other hand, almost anything, even noble descent, would impress this middle class, which had not yet won through to democratic consciousness. It felt at once the influence of a gentleman of noble birth, a *"signore di nobile istirpe e sangue."* It was impressed by anything outstanding, and it made no difference whether the distinction were military or literary, of ability, birth or wealth. In this context it is worth recalling Simmel's opinion: that when for the first time large accumulations of capital were concentrated in one hand and when the power of capital was as yet unknown to the great majority, "its influence was increased by the psychological effect of the unprecedented and the inexplicable." By its very novelty, capital, when it first appeared as a force, acted upon a set of circumstances completely alien to it "like a magic and unpredictable power." The lower classes were "bewildered by the acquisition of great wealth" and regarded its owners as "uncanny personalities." Thus it was, for example, in the case of the Grimaldi and the Medici.

This admiration for the "demoniac" we also find in the cult of *virtu*, of the man who was in any way great, which was rapidly spreading everywhere: this new type could achieve greatness only by boldly setting himself above all ethical and religious traditions and relying upon himself along with frightening boldness. Traditional morality was outmoded: even a man such as Villani, though he would morally condemn those who lacked objective virtue, could admire subjective *virtu* in them, and in his appreciation of Castruccio Castracani anticipated Machiavelli himself. Christian ethics, inasmuch as they condemned *superbia*, the complete reliance upon one's own strength, though not rejected in theory, in practice lost all influence. The individual was conscious of the fact that he had to rely completely upon his own forces. And it was the superiority of *ratio* over tradition, brought about by a mercantile age, which gave him the requisite strength. Such a penetration of all activities by the cold and calculating attitude of the merchant easily achieved a demoniac character. It was well illustrated by an entry in the ledger of the Venetian Jacopo Loredano: "The Doge Foscari: my debtor for the death of my father and uncle." And when he had removed him together with his son we find the entry "paid" on the opposite page. We see the complete repression of impulse and

the absolute control of the emotions by a ruthlessly calculating reason which inexorably moves to its goal. All this is the approach of a bourgeois age, an age of a money economy.

Money capital and mobile property naturally linked up with the kindred power of time for, seen from that particular point of view, time is money. Time is a great "liberal" power as opposed to the "conservative" power of space, the immobile soil. In the Middle Ages power belonged to him who owned the soil, the feudal lord; but now Alberti could say that he who knew how to exploit money and time fully could make himself the master of all things: such are the new means to power of the bourgeois. Money and time imply motion: "there is no more apt symbol than money to show the dynamic character of this world: as soon as it lies idle it ceases to be money in the specific sense of the word . . . the function of money is to facilitate motion" (Simmel). Money, because it circulates, as landed property cannot, shows how everything became more mobile. Money which can change one thing into another brought a tremendous amount of unrest into the world. The tempo of life was increased. Only now was formulated the new interpretation of time which saw it as a value, as something of utility. It was felt to be slipping away continuously — after the fourteenth century the clocks in the Italian cities struck all the twenty-four hours of the day. It was realized that time was always short and hence valuable, that one had to husband it and use it economically if one wanted to become the "master of all things." Such an attitude had been unknown to the Middle Ages; to them time was plentiful and there was no need to look upon it as something precious. It became so only when regarded from the point of view of the individual who could think in terms of the time measured out to him. It was scarce simply on account of natural limitations, and so everything from now on had to move quickly. For example, it became necessary to build quickly, as the patron was now building for himself. In the Middle Ages it was possible to spend tens and even hundreds of years on the completion of one building — a cathedral, a town hall or a castle (e.g. the *Certosa di Pavia* which is built in the Gothic style): for life was the life of the community in which one generation quietly succeeds another. Men lived as part of an all-embracing unity and thus life lasted long beyond its natural span. Time could be expended just as possessions or human lives themselves were. For the Middle Ages knew a hand-to-mouth economy, as was natural in an age of primary production, for agricultural produce will not keep over long periods, and the accumulation of values was thus impossible. "Where the produce of the soil is immediately consumed, a certain liberality prevails in general . . . which is less natural when money brings the desire to save" (Simmel); money will keep indefinitely. Largesse was a mediaeval virtue; Bisticci could still praise the giving of any amount "without counting the cost" and with a "liberal hand" for the "love and greater glory of God" and according to "conscience." But the splendid liberality of the Renaissance was of a totally different type. On principle it was bestowed only where it was "in place." Alberti said that "contributions towards the erection of churches and public buildings are a duty that we owe to the honour of the family and of our ancestors." Under such circumstances one gave no more than was necessary, though always as much as was seemly. The reputation of the family which could not be separated from the credit of the firm had a role of its own in the thought of the merchant. *Onesta* called for certain expenditures, but they had to prove useful and not superfluous. It would not do to be pettifogging, but the rule to spend as little as possible is the natural corollary to the rule to gain as much as possible; here is the real meaning of the specifically bourgeois virtues. An orderly plan was the rule. To make headway it was necessary to spend less or at any rate no more than one's earnings, one must treat "economically" the

body and the mind (Alberti regarded hygiene and sports as the way to strength and comeliness) and one must be industrious in contrast to the noble loafers. It was necessary to portion out time, even ration the time spent in political affairs. The Kingdom of Naples enforced over-frequent attendance at Church, and Caraccioli thought that though this might be "useful, it was most detrimental to a thorough exploitation of the day's time."

Furthermore, the merchant developed his own particular form of religiousness. The small artisan had an intimate and almost over-familiar attitude to God. The great bourgeois, on the other hand, faced him as a business partner. Giannozzo Manetti saw God as the *"maestro d'uno trafico,"* circumspectly organizing the world on the analogy of a big firm. One could open a kind of account with him, as was easily suggested by Roman Catholic emphasis on good works. Villani quite definitely regarded the giving of alms and the like as a way of securing almost by contract — the honouring of contracts is the highest virtue in the code of the honest merchant — the divine help, so that one may rely upon it. *"Ne deo quidem sine spe remunerationis servire fas est"* (Valla). Prosperity, according to Alberti, is the visible remuneration for an honest conduct of affairs pleasing to God: this is the true religious spirit of capitalism, and in a truly Roman Catholic way a kind of cooperation between grace and personal efficiency was assumed. But this "grace" was contractually due in return for one's own performance. Even religiousness became a matter for the calculation of advantages, part of a speculation designed to succeed in economic as well as political matters (cf. Villani).

The state of affairs, in fact, was that religion had ceased to be a moving force on its own and had become part of the systematized outlook of the bourgeoisie, which was primarily determined by economic considerations. The religious idea was unable fully to penetrate human life and had ceased to cause effects of any magnitude.

(The success of popular preachers of repentance was transient and sporadic.) The consciousness of belonging to a family of Western, Christian peoples, which in the Middle Ages had been upheld by knights and clergy, was alien to the bourgeoisie, taken up as it was with the feeling of national and political separations. Similarly, the class-conscious proletariat cannot recognize the bourgeois concept of the nation and the state. The living regard for Christendom or Europe taken as a whole died together with the belief in a divinely ordained duty to protect it against the infidel. The concept of a supra-national occidental community lost its meaning with the decline of those social groups which had upheld it. It now appeared outmoded and threadbare. Indeed, the idea was first abandoned by those who were called to uphold it more than anyone else, the Popes. Gregory IX and Innocent IV solicited Mahometan help against the Christian Emperor. Here too the Church, the one rational institution of the Middle Ages, had beaten the path which the Renaissance was to follow. The divers Italian states then grew accustomed to ally themselves with the Turk, "openly and unashamed" as Burckhardt has it, against the other Italian powers: "it seemed a political weapon like any other" (Burckhardt). Especially for the Italians the conception of Christian solidarity had lost all meaning; nowhere was there less dismay at the fall of Constantinople. On the contrary, an impressive personality such as Mahomet II was bound to be respected: Francesco Gonzaga, Marquess of Mantua, was prepared to address him as "friend and brother." If a Pope was asked to give aid against the Turks it was necessary to show "what advantages might accrue and what harm would be done if he were not to move." It was a Pope, Alexander VI, who did his best, in concert with Ludovico il Moro, to turn the Turks against Venice.

Religion had lost its position as a power and its function as the common bond of all to the same extent as the ruling groups of the Middle Ages had been supplanted by the bourgeoisie. Similarly national languages began to supersede Latin, the universal language of the clergy. Clerical demi-rationalism, i.e. the Thomist reconciliation of the natural and the supernatural, of the world and God, now led to complete rationalism. Religion was increasingly formalized, becoming a matter of outward observances (cf. the growing "judicial" character of religious beliefs). It was, in effect, neutralized and robbed of its hold upon life and the present. One did not go as far as to deny the theoretical possibility of divine interference by way of miracles: that was left to a later antitheist enlightenment, which by the very intransigence of its protest showed its continued or renewed preoccupation with religious problems. The typical Italian of the Renaissance was already one step further: his was that genuine atheism which has eliminated the idea of divine power from the considerations governing his actions and indeed from his thoughts and writings. Men had ceased to believe that anything irrational might intentionally interfere to disturb their own systematic designs, they thought themselves able to master *fortuna* by *virtu*. This is also shown by the absolute position that humanists assigned to the free human will. It is true that the mediaeval Church had held the doctrine of free will in matter of morality, but it deliberately maintained the theological antinomy of free will and divine grace as a religious paradox. But now in this matter too, modes of thought tending towards complete individual freedom threw off the leadership of the Church.

Social conditions which had lacked a rational basis had already given way to a systematic order. Everyone had to rely upon himself in the knowledge that neither metaphysical concepts nor supra-individual forces of the community were backing him. No longer did anyone feel himself as a trustee in office or vocation. The one goal was that of being a virtuoso; . . .

HARD TIMES AND INVESTMENT IN CULTURE

ROBERT S. LOPEZ

Robert S. Lopez was born in Italy in 1910. Educated there and in the United States, he is now Professor of History at Yale University. His publications mark him as an excellent scholar in the area of economic history, especially in medieval trade and banking. Professor Lopez presented the following paper at the Symposium on the Renaissance held at the New York Metropolitan Museum of Art on February 8–10, 1952.

WHEN humanists like Michelet and Burckhardt accredited the term Renaissance, a good many years ago, economic history had hardly been born. Their lofty reconstruction of civilization in the Renaissance was unencumbered by the suspicion that the passions of Caliban might have something to do with the achievements of Ariel. Then came the followers of Marx and historical materialism, who trimmed the wings of the poet-historians and inserted literature into the digestive process. We ought to pay our deepest respects to both schools, not only to set an example to posterity when our own turn in obsolescence comes, but also because both the brain and the stomach certainly have an influence on the movements of the heart.

Historians, however, after letting the pendulum swing fully in either direction, have labored to find an equilibrium and a chain of relations between cause and effect. The easiest way to link two unfolding developments is to describe them as parallel and interlocked at every step. The notion that wherever there was an economic peak we must also find an intellectual peak, and vice versa, has long enjoyed the unquestioned authority of mathematical postulates. In an examination book of a sophomore which I graded not so long ago, the postu-late entailed these deductions: Double-entry bookkeeping in the Medici Bank goaded Michelangelo to conceive and accomplish the Medici Chapel; contemplation of the Medici Chapel in turn spurred the bankers to a more muscular management of credit. But these statements, even if they were more skillfully worded, are quite misleading. There is no denying that many beautiful homes of the Renaissance belonged to successful businessmen — in Italy above all, then in Flanders, in southern Germany, and in other regions. Yet if bankers like the Medici and the Fuggers had been capable of conjuring up artists like Michelangelo and Dürer, then our own Rothschilds and Morgans ought to have produced bigger and better Michelangelos. And how could we explain the emergence of Goya in an impoverished Spain, or the artistic obscurity of the business metropolis that was Genoa? A minimum of subsistence is indispensable for art and a minimum of intelligence is indispensable for business. But this does not mean that great artists and great businessmen must be born in the same group and in the same generation.

What strikes us at the outset is the different relation between economy and culture in the high Middle Ages and in the Renais-

From Robert S. Lopez, "Hard Times and Investment in Culture," in *The Renaissance: A Symposium* (New York, 1953), pp. 19–32. By permission of the New York Metropolitan Museum of Art and the author.

sance. I must beg leave to begin by a very brief description of what we call the "commercial revolution" of the high Middle Ages. This great economic upheaval, comparable in size only to the modern industrial revolution, surged from the Dark Ages at about the same time as the *chansons de geste* and early Romanesque art. It reached its climax in the age of Dante and rayonnant Gothic, after which a great depression occurred. Like the modern industrial revolution, it was a period of great, continuous demographic growth, of steady if not spectacular technological progress, of expansion both through increased production and consumption at home and through conquest of new markets abroad. It was an epoch of great opportunities and great hopes, of small wars for limited objectives, and of growing toleration and interchange of ideas among persons of different classes, nations, and beliefs. Its pace was, of course, slower than that of the industrial revolution, because progress traveled by horse and galley rather than by train, steamship, and airplane. The final results, however, were probably of the same order of magnitude. The medieval commercial revolution was instrumental in bringing about the momentous changes which bequeathed to the Renaissance a society not too different from our own, and was in turn influenced by all of these changes. It caused the old feudal system to crumble and the old religious structure to weaken. It all but wiped out slavery, it gave liberty to serfs over large areas, and created a new elite based upon wealth rather than birth.

A great expansion in all other fields occurred at the same time. The blossoming of a new literature and art, the revival of science and law, the beginning of political and religious individualism, the spread of education and of social consciousness to larger strata of the population, were concurrent and contemporaneous with the commercial revolution of the high Middle Ages. Though not all facets of medieval literature and philosophy were such as one might expect of an economic expansion, who will deny that there was a connection between economic and intellectual progress? It is also proper to suggest that the economic and social change of the high Middle Ages was an indispensable preparation for the Renaissance, even as it is safe to state that a man must have been an adolescent before he can become a father. But we must not confuse two different ages. Probably there would have been no Renaissance — or, rather, the Renaissance would have taken another course — if the Middle Ages had not previously built the towns, humbled the knights, challenged the clergymen, and taught Latin grammar. But the towns of the Middle Ages created the civilization of the Middle Ages. Whether or not this civilization was as great as that of the Renaissance, it certainly was different.

Let us not say that the general coincidence of an exuberant civilization and an expansive economy in the high Middle Ages shows that great art and great business must always go together. Consider the different experience of different countries. Italy was to the medieval economic process what England was to that of the eighteenth and nineteenth centuries. It was the cradle and the pathfinder of the commercial revolution, which was on the move in several Italian towns long before it made its way through the rest of Europe. Like the industrial revolution, the commercial revolution did not spread evenly: here it passed by large areas or slackened its speed, there it gained impetus as it engulfed other generators of economic advance. In Flanders, for instance, the currents coming from Italy swelled a river which had sprung from local streams. But Ile de France, the home of so much glorious medieval art, literature, and philosophy, was a retarded if not quite a forgotten area. Its towns were small and sleepy in the shadow of the great cathedrals at a time when the Italian towns hummed with business activity and made great strides in the practical sciences of law, mathematics, and medicine, but had not yet produced a Dante, a Giotto, or an Aquinas. With these three giants Italy concluded the Middle Ages in a thoroughly medieval way. Petrarch, another Italian, ushered in the intellectual Renaissance at the very moment when the economic trend was reversed. The exact span of the Renaissance is variously measured by historians of civilization. There was a lag in time between the Renaissance in Italy and that of the other countries. Moreover, the imperialism of certain lovers of the Renaissance has led them to claim as forerunners or followers men who would be better left to the Middle Ages or to baroque. I shall assume that, chronologically speaking, the Renaissance means roughly the period between 1330 and 1530, though the economic picture would not substantially change if we added a few decades at the beginning or at the end. Now that period was not one of economic expansion. It was one of great depression followed by a moderate and incomplete recovery.

Time alone will tell whether the economy of the age in which we live is the early stage of another "Renaissance" rather than the prelude to another "Dark Age," or a mere pause before another cycle of expansion. We shall see in a moment that certain resemblances seem to bring the Renaissance closer to us than any other historical period, in the economic field as in many others. But there was no resemblance in regard to population trends. Following a great plunge in the mid-fourteenth century, the population of Europe tended to stagnate at a far lower level than that of the high Middle Ages. A number of epidemics, far more terrible than any medieval contagion, whittled down the population. Famines, birth control, and other causes which cannot be enumerated here even in the most summary fashion, contributed to the same end. The decline was particularly pronounced in cities — the very homes of the essentially urban civilization that was the Renaissance. The country suffered less and recovered better, but it did not escape the general pattern.

The falling curve of the population was to some extent connected with other retarding factors. Technological progress continued, but, with the notable exceptions of the insurance contract, the printing press and certain advances in metallurgy, it was represented by diffusion and improvement of medieval methods and tools rather than by the invention of new ones. True, there was Leonardo da Vinci; but his amazing inventions were of no avail to his contemporaries, who were uninformed and probably uninterested in them. Again, the Renaissance introduced a better type of humanistic schools and of education for the elite, but it made no sweeping changes in technical education and no significant advances in bringing literacy to the masses. In these respects the Renaissance was less "modern" than the high Middle Ages.

A closer resemblance to our own times lies in the fact that the gradual shrinking of political horizons frustrated the improved means of transportation and the powerful organization of international trade which the Middle Ages had bequeathed to the Renaissance. Shortly before the Renaissance began, a Florentine merchant had described the road from the Crimea to Peking as perfectly safe to westerners — a statement which we would hesitate to make today. But, during the Renaissance, East and West were split deeply, first by the collapse of the Mongolian Empire in the Far and Middle East, then by the Turkish conquest in the Near East. A medieval advance in the opposite direction was nullified before its possibilities were grasped: the Scandinavians abandoned Vinland, Greenland, and Iceland. Within Europe each state manifested its incipient centralization by raising economic barriers against all of the others. To be sure, the twilight of the Renaissance was lighted up by the greatest geographic discoveries. But it was a long time before the beneficial effects of the new round of discoveries were felt. The first telling result was the disruptive revolution of prices through the flood of American silver and gold — and even this came when the Renaissance had already been seized by its gravediggers, the Reformation and the Counter-Reformation.

War and inflation were as familiar to the Renaissance as they are, unfortunately, to us. It is true that already in the high Middle Ages a continuous but gradual and moderate inflation of the coinage and a parallel growth of credit money had provided much needed fuel for the demographic and economic expansion of the commercial revolution. But in the Renaissance inflation was steeper and steeper. Soft money did not supply larger means of payment for a growing number of producers and consumers. It was chiefly turned out by monarchies and city-states to pay for the largest wars that had afflicted Europe since the fall of the Roman world — the largest that Europe was to witness before the Napoleonic period, or perhaps our own world wars. One thinks first of the Hundred Years War, which, with some intermediate truces, lasted well over a century and plagued most of western Europe. The Angevin-Aragonese contest was smaller in scope, but it desolated the whole of southern Italy and Sicily for almost two hundred years. The Turkish armies inflicted still greater sufferings upon southeastern and east-central Europe. In northern Italy the mercenaries may have been gentle when fighting one another, but they were a plague to private harvests and public treasuries. Germany was the theatre of incessant local wars and brigandage, and Spain was hardly more peaceful. It is true that in the second half of the fifteenth century most of Europe had some respite. But then came the wars between the Hapsburgs and France, with intervention of the Turks, which involved the whole of Europe, used artillery on a large scale, and renewed atrocities that had almost disappeared in the high Middle Ages. They had not ended when the wars of religion began.

Needless to say, disease and famine were faithful companions of war. Moreover, during the fourteenth century desperate revolts of peasants and city proletarians burst out almost everywhere from England to the Balkans and from Tuscany to Flanders. They also claimed their victims. In the fifteenth century a dull resignation seemed to prevail and banditism sprouted — sometimes even in the vicinity of towns. The early sixteenth century was marred by terrible peasants' revolts in Hungary, Germany, northeastern Italy, Switzerland, and northern France.

Then, as now, inflation was not enough to support the burden of war. Taxation rose to much higher levels than during the commercial revolution, when a booming economy could have borne it more easily. It fleeced peasants and landlords, but it skinned the bourgeoisie, which had greater amounts of cash. In France and England the Renaissance marked the downfall of town autonomy, largely though not exclusively because the towns were unable to balance their budgets and because the richer bourgeois, who could have come to the assistance of their poorer fellow-citizens, refused to bear even their own full share. In Italy the independent towns survived, at a price. They fell under dictators, who brought about some equalization of burdens through universal oppression; or under small oligarchies of very rich men, who could either bear or evade taxation.

Yet it would not be fair to ascribe to taxation alone the principal blame for an economic recession which was essentially caused by shrinking or dull markets. The markets had shrunk because the population had diminished or stagnated, and because the frontier had receded and had been locked up. Perhaps some compensation would have been found through a better distribution of wealth if the scattered revolts of the fourteenth century had grown into a general social revolution. They failed. The recurrence of wars and epidemics throttled whatever social ferment remained in the fifteenth century. In the general stagnation some of the rich men grew richer, many of the poor men grew poorer, and the others at best obtained security at the expense of opportunity.

The ominous signs are visible everywhere. Land prices and landlords' profits in the Renaissance were at their lowest ebb in centuries. The great movement of land reclamation and colonization which had characterized the centuries between the tenth and the early fourteenth was arrested. As early as the thirteenth century, to be sure, many landlords in England, in Spain, in southern Italy, and in northwestern France had transformed arable land into sheep ranges. Wool was a good cash crop and sheep farming required little manpower. The process continued throughout the Renaissance, but it became less and less rewarding as the demand for wool became stagnant or declined. Great patches of marginal and even fairly good land, which had been exploited in the Middle Ages, were now returned to waste. Fertile estates were sold or rented for nominal prices. But even these low prices were too high for many hungry, landless peasants who lacked even the small capital needed to buy seeds and tools. Fortunate was the peasant whose lord was willing to advance money in return for a share in the crop.

In the high Middle Ages the towns had absorbed not only an ever increasing amount of foodstuffs and industrial raw materials, but also the surplus product of the human plant. Noblemen, yeomen, and serfs, each one according to his capacity, could then easily find occupation and advancement in town. In the Renaissance, opportunities were usually reserved for those who were citizens of the town. Yet citizens, too, had little chance to improve their lot. The guilds formerly had accepted apprentices freely and assured every apprentice of the opportunity of becoming a master. Now they became rigid hierarchies; only the son of a master could hope to succeed to the mastership. Outsiders were either rejected or kept permanently in the subordinate position of journeymen. This trend also affected the guilds of artists. Occasionally, to be sure, a town encouraged immigration of qualified groups of countrymen on condition that they carry out the humbler industrial tasks at lower salaries than those of the lowest journeymen. Again, the old practice of putting out raw materials for peasants to work at home gained some ground, but the increase of manufacturing in the country fell far short of compensating for the decrease of industrial production in towns. It was not a symptom of economic growth but merely a means of depressing wages. Luxury industries alone maintained and perhaps increased their production. This reflects the decline of production for the masses and the growing distance between the very rich and the very poor.

The growing dullness of European markets and the loss of many eastern markets was bound to depress commerce. The leitmotif now was to offer for sale, not the greatest quantity and variety of goods, but — to quote a fifteenth-century manual of business — "only as much as one can sell in the place of destination." Nor was it always possible to buy as much as one desired. Wars and embargoes frequently interfered with trade. Increased duties in nearly every country from England to Egypt raised the cost of many wares to prohibitive heights. The age of rapid fortunes won in daring oversea and overland ventures was over. Sedentary merchants could still maintain their position if they employed many able and loyal employees and commission agents, if they planned every step carefully, and if they could wait patiently for their investments to bring hard-won profits. In Italy five to eight per cent was now regarded as a fair interest in commercial loans — a much lower rate than those prevailing in the high Middle Ages, although risks had not diminished. Banks improved their methods and often increased their size while diminishing in numbers. But they had to use a larger and larger proportion of their capital not for trade but for loans to the idle upper class and more frequently to belligerent states. Such investments usually brought high interest for a very short period and failure when the debtor was unable to pay the principal.

One business — insurance — boomed during the Renaissance. It bordered on gambling. Investors had no statistics to rely upon. Risky speculations on foreign exchange also drained capital away from commercial investments. Overt gambling attracted ambitious men who despaired of other gainful occupations. There were the extreme cases of scoundrels who staked their money against the life of an unknowing person and had that person murdered so that they could cash the bet. At the other extremity were many business men who abandoned trade and invested in land, not merely a part of their capital, as merchants had always done, but everything they had. Even when bought at the lowest prices, land was not very remunerative; but it could insure some reward for the owner who sank enough money in improvements and administered the investment in the spirit of business. The shift of production from butter to guns was reflected in the different fortune of merchants who exploited mines. After a long slump in mining there was a sudden boom in the late fifteenth and early sixteenth centuries. Metallurgy prospered: iron and bronze were war materials, and precious metals were the sinews of war. They also were needed to pay tributes to the Turks and increased custom duties to the Egyptians. But alum, a basic material for the declining cloth industry, was not in great demand. When the mines increased their output, the price of alum fell.

Italy, the earliest and most brilliant center of the artistic Renaissance, felt the impact of the economic recession most heavily. Its condition resembled somewhat that of England after 1918, or that of New England after 1929. Italy fell harder because it had climbed higher. It had exploited most of its possibilities, and it could not seek recovery by opening up many new fields of enterprise. Conversely, those countries which watered down their intellectual Renaissance with the largest proportion of medieval strains also seem to have felt the shock of the economic crisis less deeply.

Of course, we must not overstress the dark side of the picture. Contraction and stagnation had succeeded expansion, but the economic ceiling of the fifteenth century was still much higher than the top level of the twelfth, though it was lower than the peak of the thirteenth. The bourgeoisie preserved its commanding position in Italy and its influence in the western monarchies. The amazing progress of the commercial revolution in methods and techniques was not lost; indeed, the depression spurred business men to further rationalization and sounder management. Thanks to their accumulated experience and capital, the Italians not only defended their leading position but also quickened the recovery of other countries by investing capital and frequently establishing their residence abroad. Some countries which had formerly been retarded felt the full impact of the commercial revolution only now.

Finally, the depression and even the greatest disasters were sources of profit for some men. In many places food prices declined faster than real wages. Cheap land and cheap manpower made the fortune of many entrepreneurs. War enabled Jacques Coeur to grab fabulous riches. Inflation was a boon to the Fuggers, who controlled silver and copper mines. Southern Germany gained from the disruption of communications through France and, later, from the ruin of Venetian and Florentine banks. Barcelona inherited some of the trade which had slipped from Pisa. Antwerp fell heir to the commerce, though not to the industry, of other Flemish towns. Some of these successes were fleeting. Others lasted as long as the Renaissance. None of them, however, was as durable as had been the commercial and industrial blossoming of Italy and Belgium or the prime of English and French agriculture in the high Middle Ages. Qualitatively and quantitatively the compensations fell short of the deficiencies.

Economic historians are usually expected to back their statement with figures. These are not easily tested for a period which had not yet learned how to use statistics for the information of friends and the misinformation of enemies. Still what statistical data we have are reliable enough as indications of trends in growth or decrease, if not as absolute indexes of size. Here are some figures:

In 1348 the population of England was at least 3,700,000. In the early fifteenth century it plunged as low as 2,100,000. Then it rose slowly, but as late as 1545 it was still half a million short of the pre-Renaissance level. Yet England suffered comparatively little from war, and presumably was less affected by the economic slump than were some more advanced countries. Again, Florence in the time of Dante had more than 100,000 inhabitants, but no more than 70,000 in the time of Boccaccio, and approximately the same number in the time of Michelangelo. Zürich, a typical middle-size town, fell from 12,375 inhabitants in 1350 to 4,713 in 1468. Similar declines can be measured for the larger part of towns and countries. As for the often cited compensating factors, Antwerp, the one Belgian town whose population increased in the Renaissance while that of all the others decreased, in 1526 had 8,400 houses. There still were as many houses in Bruges, its ruined rival. Again, Catalonia, one of the few countries which continued to grow after the early fourteenth century, rose from 87,000 to 95,000 homesteads from 1359 to 1365. But it declined to 59,000 in 1497, and it was still down at 75,000 in 1553.

To turn to another kind of figures, the incoming and outgoing wares subject to tax in the port of Genoa were valued at £3,822,000 Genoese in 1293. The figure fell to £887,000 in 1424. In 1530 it was still more than one million short of the 1293 level, in spite of the fact that the purchasing power of the pound had greatly declined in the interval. Again, the aggregate capital of the main house and seven of the eight branches of the Medici bank in 1458 was less than 30,000 florins,

whereas the capital of the Peruzzi bank in the early fourteenth century had risen above the 100,000 florin mark. Yet the Medici company in the Renaissance towered above all other Florentine companies, whereas the medieval Peruzzi company was second to that of the Bardi. Similarly, the combined fortunes of the three richest members of the Medici family in 1460 were valued at only fifteen per cent more than the fortune of one Alberti merchant a hundred years earlier. As for the so-called compensating factors, it is true that in 1521 Jakob Fugger the Rich obtained from Emperor Charles V an acknowledgment of debt for 600,000 florins. But in the early fourteenth century the English king owed the Bardi company an equal sum, according to English documents, which probably underestimated the debt, or 900,000 florins according to Villani, who may have overestimated it. In addition, the English king owed the Peruzzi company a sum two thirds as large.

The woolen industry affords the best examples in regard to manufacturing because it worked chiefly for an international market. Without leaving Florence, we note that in 1378 the weavers went on strike to demand of the industrialists that they should pledge a minimum yearly output of 24,000 pieces of cloth. Forty years earlier the yearly output had been between 70,000 and 80,000 pieces. Yet the depression did not hit Florence as hard as Flanders, her greater rival. The slow growth of English woolen industry, which occurred at the same period, was far from compensating the decline of production in the other major centers. Total export figures very seldom exceeded 50,000 pieces, and usually were not higher than 30,000.

It is harder to put one's finger upon agrarian figures. But we may regard as suitable examples the contraction of cultivated areas and the falling prices of agricultural products in a time of general monetary inflation. In Prussia the price of rye fell by almost two thirds between 1399 and 1508. In England the price of grain declined by forty seven per cent between 1351 and 1500, and that of cattle and animal products declined by thirty-two per cent. "Of the 450 odd [English] manors for which the fifteenth-century accounts have been studied, over 400 show a contraction of land in the hands of tenants." In Gascony after 1453 "thirty per cent of the rural villages were ravaged or seriously damaged." The plain of southern Tuscany, which had been reclaimed in the high Middle Ages, now relapsed to its previous condition of a malaria-ridden waste. In Castile the most powerful company of sheep owners in 1477 owned 2,700,000 sheep, or roughly a sheep for every other inhabitant of the country. Figures of this kind, and the frequent reports about starvation and vagrancy, more than offset what information we have on agricultural progress in some parts of Lombardy and the introduction of some new plants to France.

I hope I have said enough to show that the Renaissance was neither an economic golden age nor a smooth transition from moderate medieval well-being to modern prosperity. I have fired only a small part of the available ammunition; still less would have been needed but for the fact that the newer findings of economic historians do not easily pierce the crust of preconceived impressions. Is it necessary to add that nobody should jump to the opposite conclusion and contend that the coincidence of economic depression and artistic splendor in the Renaissance proves that art is born of economic decadence? I do not think it is. We have just seen that the peak of medieval economy coincided with the zenith of medieval art.

A more insidious path would be open to straight economic determinism if someone invoked the overwrought theory of cultural lags. Cultural lags, as everybody knows, are ingenious, elastic devices to link together events which cannot be linked by any other means. Someone might suggest that a cultural lag bridged the gap between the economic high point of the thirteenth century and the intellectual high point of the fif-

teenth, so that the intellectual revolution of the Renaissance was a belated child of the commercial revolution of the Middle Ages. What should one answer? Personally, I doubt the paternity of children who were born two hundred years after the death of their fathers. To be sure, the Renaissance utilized for its development the towns which the Middle Ages had built, the philosophy which the Greeks had elaborated, and nearly everything else that mankind had contrived ever since Neanderthal; but its way of life was conditioned by its own economy and not by the economy of the past.

There is no heap of riches and no depth of poverty that will automatically insure or forbid artistic achievement. Intellectual developments must be traced primarily to intellectual roots. But that does not at all mean that they are independent of economic conditions. The connection is not a direct and crude relation of cause and effect. It is a complicated harmony in which innumerable economic factors and innumerable cultural factors form together a still greater number of chords. That some of them are incongruous or dissonant should not surprise us. Every age is full of contradictions.

We have a unison rather than an accord when the literature and the art of the Renaissance make direct allusions to the troubled economic circumstances. Machiavelli in his *History of Florence* is well aware of the crisis, its causes and its manifestations. Martin Luther inveighs against the consequences of economic causes which he does not clearly perceive. The anonymous author of *Lazarillo de Tormes* embraces in his sympathetic irony the disinherited of all social classes. Agrippa d'Aubigné described in Biblical terms the terrible sufferings of France. Donatello and Jerome Bosch crowd their bas-reliefs and their paintings with portraits of starved persons. The enumeration could continue, but it would bring little light to the interrelation of economics and culture. What we look for is not the direct image of economic facts, but the indirect repercussions of these facts on the development of ideas.

Of the many connections that might be suggested, some are too far-fetched and dubious for an earthly economic historian to take stock of them. For instance, some clever contrivance might be found to link together economic rationalization and intellectual rationalism. One might compare the clarity and symmetry of Renaissance double-entry books of accounting to the clarity and symmetry of Renaissance buildings. But the Renaissance also created such poems as that of Ariosto, which is anything but symmetrical, and such philosophies as that of Marsilio Ficino, which is anything but clear. Moreover, double-entry accounting was not a monopoly of the Renaissance. It made its first appearance in the early fourteenth century, if not earlier, and it is still used today. Perhaps we should leave these lofty comparisons to the examination book which I cited at the beginning.

More definite connections probably existed between specific economic factors and some themes or fashions in the literature, art, and thought of the Renaissance. Consider, for instance, the theme of the Wheel of Fortune, which is one of the refrains of the age. To be sure, the blind goddess at all times has exercised her influence upon all forms of human activity. But her sway has seldom been as capricious and decisive as in the Renaissance, when gambling was one of the principal means of making a fortune, and when ill fortune alone could unseat the fortunate few who were sitting pretty. Then consider the vogue of pastoral romance and the fresh interest in country life. The country always has its fans and its idealizers. Still its charm must have been particularly alluring to merchants who returned to the country after generations of rush to the city. They found there not only a better investment but also a healthier atmosphere and a more sincere way of life. Again, the list could easily be lengthened, but it might seem an anti-climax to those who are waiting for a comprehensive interpretation of the interplay of economy as a

whole and culture as a whole. I shall not attempt to concoct a catch-all formula, which would only conceal the endless variety of actions and reactions. No harm is done, however, if the discordant details are grouped in tentative generalizations.

We have seen that the essential phases of Renaissance economy were first a depression, then stabilization at a lower level than the highest medieval summit. The implicit opposition between those two trends, depression and stabilization, may perhaps help us to understand a certain dualism in the general outlook of the Renaissance. Note that I said "may help to explain," not "explain." I am not postulating direct causes, but what my brilliant colleague, Mr. Ferguson, would call "permissive or partially effective causes." Some Renaissance men were pessimists: they thought of the lost heights rather than of the attained platform. Others, especially those who had managed to settle down in sufficient comfort, felt that they had definitely and finally arrived.

The pessimists may not have been the larger group, but they seem to have included some of the most significant personalities, ranging from Savonarola to Machiavelli, from Leonardo da Vinci to Michelangelo, from Dürer to Cervantes, from Thomas More perhaps to William Shakespeare. It would be useless to list more names without accounting for their inclusion, but I may be allowed, as an economic historian, to point out some of the intellectual aspects of depression. Some pessimists joined the medieval preachers in demanding an earnest return to God, or they imitated the pagan writers in exalting the golden age of primitive mankind. Others maintained that all human history, or indeed the history of the universe, is a succession of cycles in growth and decay, with no hope for permanent progress. Still others built political theories upon the assumption that men are basically gullible and corrupt, and that a statesman must adapt his strategy to human imperfection. Similar assumptions underlay many tragedies, comedies, and novels. Quite a few pessimists voiced the plight of the poor and the weak, or portrayed them in the background — but seldom in the forefront, because the forefront was reserved for the rich and the strong who purchased the work of art. A number invoked death or sleep, the brother of death. A larger number sought an escape from reality, not in Heaven but in a world of artistic, literary, philosophical, or even mathematical dreams. All of these diverse trends may of course be detected during any historical period, but they seem more pronounced during the Renaissance. It is easier to link them with economic depression than with any other economic trend.

The optimists in the Renaissance were not as different from the pessimists as one might think at first. Usually they shared with the pessimists a widespread belief in the flow and ebb of civilization, and a tendency to look for an ideal of perfection in the past and not in the future. Their standard, however, was nothing like the coarse emotionalism of the Middle Ages or the naïve primitiveness of the mythical Golden Age. It was classic antiquity — another age of stability and poise in aristocratic refinement. The optimists thought that antiquity had been one of the high tides in human history, and that their own time was another high tide, intimately close to antiquity and utterly unrelated to the recent past. Now was the time to stretch one's hand for the riches which the high tide brought within reach. One could be Horatian and pluck the rose of youth and love before her beauty had faded. One could be more ambitious and make every effort to comprehend, fulfil, and enjoy the greater wealth which was now accessible to men freed from instinct and ignorance. Private individuals and political leaders were equally impatient. Their drive for self-fulfillment was humanitarian and peaceful so long as they strove to discover and develop their own self, their own moral and material resources. But it had to become aggressive individualism and political ruthlessness

when success depended upon conquest of resources claimed by other individuals or nations. All of these characteristics, too, can be found in other ages, but they seem to predominate in the Renaissance. They are not surprising in an economic stagnation which still offers a good life to the elite but little hope for the outcast.

The moods of the Renaissance are so many and so various that they seem almost to defy definition. That is exactly why the Renaissance looks so modern to us — it was almost as rich and diversified as the contemporary scene. One important modern trait, however, was lacking. Most of its exponents had little faith and little interest in progress for the whole human race. Indeed this idea seems to be germane to economic expansion. The religious ideal of progress of mankind from the City of Man towards the City of God hardly survived the end of the commercial revolution and the failure of social revolts in the fourteenth century. In the later period, even the most pious men tended to exclude forever from the City of God the infidel, the heretic, and frequently all but a handful of Catholic ascetics or Protestant militant men predestined for salvation. The secular ideal of progress of mankind through the diffusion of decency and learning was seldom emphasized before the late sixteenth century, when economic stagnation began at last to be broken. In between there were nearly two hundred years — the core of the Renaissance — during which any hope for progress was generally held out, not to the vulgar masses but to individual members of a small elite, not to the unredeemable "barbarians" but to the best representatives of chosen peoples.

Contrary to widespread popular belief, the society of the Renaissance was essentially aristocratic. It offered economic, intellectual, and political opportunities to only a small number. But it lacked a universally accepted standard of nobility. The commercial revolution of the high Middle Ages and the social changes connected with it already had undermined the aristocracy of blood. The great depression of the mid-fourteenth century, and the stagnation which followed shook the security and whittled down the income of the aristocracy of wealth. Blood and money, of course, were still very useful — they always are — but neither insured durable distinction by itself. Too many landowners, merchants, and bankers had lost or were threatened with losing their wealth, and high birth without wealth was of little avail in the age which has been called "the heyday of illegitimate children." Neither was there any recognized hierarchy of states and nations. The Holy Roman Empire of the Germanic people had fallen to pieces; the Papacy had come close to total dissolution; France and England rose and fell many times; the Italian city-states witnessed a stunning series of *coups d'état* and mutations of fortune.

Perhaps this was why culture, what we still call humanistic culture, tended to become the highest symbol of nobility, the magic password which admitted a man or a nation to the elite group. Its value rose at the very moment that the value of land fell. Its returns mounted when commercial interest rates declined. Statesmen who had tried to build up their power and prestige by enlarging their estates now vied with one another to gather works of art. Business men who had been looking for the most profitable or the most conservative investments in trade now invested in books. The shift was more pronounced in Italy because in Italy business men and statesmen were the same persons. And it is in this field, I believe, that we can most profitably investigate the relation between economic and intellectual trends of the Renaissance. We ought to explore briefly the increased value of humanistic culture as an economic investment.

Quite probably the increase was relative and not absolute. It is doubtful that the Renaissance invested in humanistic culture more than any period of the Middle Ages. The precious metals which early medieval artists lavished in their works were a staggering proportion of the available stocks of gold and silver. The cathedrals and castles of the twelfth century probably absorbed a greater amount of raw materials and man-power-hours than the churches and palaces of the Renaissance. Medieval universities were far greater investments, in strictly economic terms, than the humanistic schools. But universities, cathedrals and castles were not built primarily — or, at least, not exclusively — for the sake of pure humanistic culture. Universities aimed at preparing men for professional careers, such as those of clergyman, lawyer, and physician. Castles were insurances against accidents in this life. It is not surprising that shrewd rulers and thrifty business men were prepared to invest part of their capital in functional works of art and in practical culture.

The investment, however, often was inversely proportional to the intensity of business spirit. We have noted that northern France, the home of most of the largest cathedrals, was one of the retarded countries in the commercial revolution. Let us now point out that cathedrals in northern Italy and Tuscany were usually smaller than those of France. Paris had the largest faculty of theology, whereas Italian universities stressed the more practical studies of law and medicine. Genoa, perhaps the most businesslike town in medieval Italy, had one of the smallest cathedrals and no university at all. Yet its inhabitants were pious and its merchants were quite cultured. Very many had gone to business schools and a good number had been graduated from a law school. But the state was run as a business proposition — and good management warned against immobilizing too many resources in humanistic culture, which was functional only to a limited extent.

The evolution from the state as a business affair to the state as a work of art, if I may still use the Burckhardtian formula, went together with the depression and the stagnation of the Renaissance. The decline of aristocracy and the recession of plutocracy left a gap through which culture, that other noblesse, could more easily shine. That culture was placed so high — higher, perhaps, than at any other period in history — is the undying glory of the Renaissance.

The transition was smooth because the seeds had been planted in the high Middle Ages. Already in the thirteenth century, culture was a creditable pastime to the nobleman and a useful asset to the merchant. It was then the fashion for kings and courtiers to write elegant lyric poems — or to have them written by the Robert Sherwoods of the time — on very subtle matters of love and courtship. So did the merchants who traded in and ruled over the Italian towns. They did still more: they elaborated a formula which vaguely anticipated the Renaissance notion that humanistic culture is the true noblesse. Real love, polite love — they said — can dwell only in a gentle heart. Though a gentle heart is not yet the well-rounded personality of the Renaissance, it resembles it in at least two ways. It is unconnected with birth or riches, and it is attainable by cultivating one's soul. Again, the Italian bourgeois of the thirteenth century were not content with building substantial houses with capacious storage rooms for their merchandise and with high towers from which to pour boiling oil on the lower towers of their neighbors. They embellished their homes as much as they could without diminishing the width of the storage rooms and the height of the towers. But a merchant of the thirteenth century would have been ill advised if he had neglected the expanding opportunities of trade for the pursuit of humanistic culture. He was too busy making money to consider lyric poetry and home decoration as a full-time occupation.

During the Renaissance many merchants were less busy — or, at least, thought they could spare more time for culture. In 1527 a Venetian merchant and ambassador was somewhat shocked at seeing that in Florence "men who govern the Republic sort and sift wool, and their sons sell cloth and engage in other work including the lowest and dirtiest." But this race of men was gradually dying out in Florence, as it had in Venice. More frequently the Italian

merchant princes of the Renaissance had employees and correspondents who did the dirtier work for them.

Let us take a great merchant, indeed the head of the world's greatest financial organization in the fifteenth century, Lorenzo the Magnificent. He was at the same time the head of the Medici bank, the uncrowned king of Florence, a patron of art, and a poet in his own right. His record shows that, unlike his medieval forefathers, he was an amateur in business and a professional in literature. His mismanagement of the bank, or, rather, the mismanagement of the men he intrusted with running it, precipitated its downfall. But his patronage of the arts gave his illegitimate power a halo of respectability. His poems endeared him to his subjects — at least, to those who had not been involved in the failure of the bank — and made him famous among intellectual aristocrats throughout the world. Niccolo Machiavelli, the great historian of Florence, lauded Lorenzo for governing the state as an artist but blamed him for his poor conduct of business. Yet was this shortcoming not the inevitable counterpart of his artistic achievements? Today we no longer suffer from the ruin of the Medici bank, while we still are enchanted by the verse of Lorenzo de Medici. It is easier for us to be indulgent and to observe that business at that time was so bad that even a skillful management would not have brought many dividends. Perhaps Lorenzo may be forgiven for overlooking some opportunities to invest in trade at five per cent interest since he invested in art at a rate which will never be exhausted.

One might even contend that investment in culture drove the Renaissance to untimely death. To obtain money for the building of Saint Peter's in Rome, the only Renaissance church that probably represented a greater investment in material and manpower than any of the Gothic cathedrals, Pope Leo X — another Medici — proclaimed a special indulgence. The sale of indulgences was the spark which ignited the Reformation. . . .

COMMUNICATIONS TO THE EDITOR OF
THE AMERICAN HISTORICAL REVIEW

R. S. LOPEZ AND HANS BARON

To the Editor of the American Historical Review:

Before taking issue with Professor Hans Baron in connection with his review of Professor Labande's *L'Italie de la Renaissance* (AHR, January, 1956, pp. 385–87), I want to stress that I value very highly everything that comes from his pen, including the review. But I am not fully convinced by his definitions of what he calls "les données essentielles" of the problem, that is, presumably, the uncontrovertible generalizations upon which all works should be based.

Since economic history is the field with which I am more familiar, I shall limit my remarks to it. Professor Baron's objection to Labande's "assertion of an all-engulfing economic decay" would find little support with the majority of economic historians — unless, of course, "all-engulfing" means "total and unrelieved," which is a far more radical position than Labande's. For instance, in the latest general work on the subject, *Cambridge Economic History of Europe*, II (1952), several scholars of two countries, each of them writing without contact with the others, agreed in a verdict of general decline. Much the same outlook prevailed in the Third International Convention of Renaissance Studies (Florence, 1952) and at the Tenth International Congress of Historical Sciences (Rome, 1955), albeit in both cases there were expressions of dissent and many qualifications. That every generalization must be qualified is a truism which should not impair the validity of the generalization. Thus, in the face of

a widely documented demographic stagnation or regression, it does not seem vitally important that "marriages and births did not decline everywhere" (incidentally, of the four authorities quoted by Baron to this effect Barbagallo was a supporter of the decay theory, von Beloch had no figures for the Middle Ages, and Pieri is a political, not an economic, historian; moreover, Fernand Braudel is probably the greatest specialist of early modern economic history, but his research has never gone farther back than 1492). As for the fact that "public debt in Venice and Milan decreased," the identification of prosperity with balanced budgets is not a bipartisan economic dogma. There are those who will be more impressed by the collapse of nearly all Venetian banks and by the fatal inadequacy of Milanese military expenditures.

Without going into further detail I would like to submit that there is a cultural lag between the findings of economic historians and those of political or intellectual historians. The lag is unfortunately broadened by the fact that the latter would prefer to believe in a great economic upswing to sustain the intellectual blossoming of the Renaissance. Who knows? Further research in economic history may in the future give them some comfort. But until and unless this happens, we have to take stock of the now prevalent theory that the Renaissance witnessed a deep economic crisis though not a total catastrophe (are there any total catastrophes in history?), and that in spite

From "Communication," *The American Historical Review*, LXI (1956), pp. 1087–89. By permission of the editor of *The American Historical Review*.

of many local, partial, or temporary gains it represented an anticlimax or at least a phase of slower development after the quicker progress of the medieval commercial revolution. Naturally this should not prevent Professor Baron's siding with the minority of economic historians who deny the existence of the crisis — provided he warns the reader that is only a minority opinion.   ROBERT SABATINO LOPEZ

TO THE EDITOR OF THE AMERICAN HISTORICAL REVIEW:

I am glad that Professor Lopez in such a friendly and generous fashion broaches a problem that has troubled me since, in the "Renaissance Symposium" of the Metropolitan Museum of Art in 1952, he first made "preconceived impressions" responsible for widespread hesitation to subscribe to the theory that the economic depression which started with the fourteenth century continued in the Italy of the Quattrocento. In his stimulating Symposium paper, Lopez argued: under the impact of the retrogression, even in Italy areas previously cultivated were abandoned; economic freedom decreased as guilds were closed to newcomers; the rich grew richer and the poor, poorer; and these experiences influenced Renaissance thought, by engendering pessimism, as in Machiavelli, and a belief in a cyclical flow and ebb of culture.

Is this provocative theory, either *in toto* or in part, shared by the majority of present-day economic historians? From their published statements it would be impossible to gain this impression. The only extant comprehensive descriptions of the economic situation in Renaissance Italy, by G. Luzzatto and C. Barbagallo, revised as late as 1955 and 1952, include a wealth of evidence not only of successful Quattrocento compensations for fourteenth-century losses in banking, trade, and industry, but also of extension and amelioration of the cultivated land — a definite expansion of Italian agriculture after 1400, as C. M. Cipolla has recently maintained. Domination of economic life through the guilds, according to Luzzatto, was weakened by "una tendenza verso una maggiore libertà economica" than had existed before the Quattrocento and was to exist after 1550. According to Barbagallo, the Quattrocento saw a "wider diffusion of medium fortunes" than had been known previously; and if we follow the account of the conditions of the industrial and agricultural workers by P. S. Leicht (1946), we have no reason to assume a lowering of wages in purchase power. As for the "decay" recognized by Barbagallo, he was thinking essentially of the economic destruction caused by the wars of the late Renaissance after the 1480's; and even there he may have exaggerated the decline, as I have pointed out in *Bibl. d'Hum. et Ren. XVII* (1955), 433 f. Regarding "the collapse of nearly all Venetian banks" in the 1490's, V. Magalhães-Godinho (*Eventail . . . à L. Febvre*, 1953) has suggested that the causes lay largely not in Venice's public finance but in temporary trade conditions in the East; and the catastrophe was followed by an impressive Venetian reconstruction, which is also known through P. Sardella's research.

At the Ninth International Congress of Historical Sciences in 1950, a joint report of four economic historians (Cipolla, Dhondt, Postan, Ph. Wolff) acknowledged that in North and Central Italy the rural population and the agricultural output rose after 1400. And at the Tenth Congress, in 1955, a five-man report (by Mollat, Postan, P. Johansen, Sapori, Verlinden) warned that the assumption of a continued depression during the fifteenth century everywhere in Europe might lure us into a "snare"; according to present knowledge, Italy, after having led "la première renaissance économique" during the twelfth century, in the Quattrocento "aurait inauguré la seconde, tandis que le reste de l'Occident connaissait encore la dépression."

HANS BARON

TOWARD A MORE POSITIVE EVALUATION OF THE FIFTEENTH-CENTURY RENAISSANCE: *Part II*

HANS BARON

The selection which follows is a continuation of an article previously introduced. In Part I (page 35) Dr. Baron examined some of the political contributions of the Renaissance to the modern state; here he presents his views on the contributions of the Quattrocento to the development of modern science.

THESE observations in the field of political history will help to unravel the apparent contradictions confronting us in the history of Quattrocento science. Virtually all the recent re-interpretations of phases of intellectual life in the fourteenth, fifteenth, and sixteenth centuries, to which Professor Durand refers in his memoir, have used one standard of evaluation — the question how much the authors and schools of thought studied contributed to the rise of modern natural science. But to the humanist Renaissance of the fourteenth and fifteenth centuries interest in natural science, however fundamental to the modern world, was as unfamiliar as the institutions of the modern nation-state. Natural science was the one great sector of intellectual activity that was almost wholly excluded from the humanistic program for almost a century and a half, in favor of the new study of man and history. It is in accord with this fact that Burckhardt based his evaluation of the fifteenth century on no excessive claims for any originality in the field of science. Partly for these, partly for personal reasons, he largely omitted science from his *Civilization of the Renaissance in Italy* — as did most of the subsequent accounts of the period. Only in monographic contributions to the history of the sciences has an attempt been made to establish "primacies" for the fifteenth century in positive science also — primacies outside the humanistic movement, notably of Toscanelli in Florence and of the Averroism of Padua. These studies in fifteenth-century science, long impaired by chauvinistic prejudices, as Dr. Durand has pointed out, have recently received an objective critical revision, largely through the efforts of American scholars. Closer investigation — particularly such as made by Professors Thorndike and Randall — has shown that in fact no startling innovations were made before the end of the fifteenth century, although the ban on science by humanists did not prevent studies of the medieval type from being continued throughout the Quattrocento. But when these statements are made, what does this mean for the validity of Burckhardt's picture? Apparently no errors of perspective have been detected in his analysis, but a much broader basis has been made available

From Hans Baron, "Toward a More Positive Evaluation of the Fifteenth-Century Renaissance," in the *Journal of the History of Ideas*, IV (1943), 27–49. By permission of the editors of the *Journal of the History of Ideas*.

for re-examining the meaning of the humanist disregard of science and of the cursory treatment of this sector of intellectual life in many modern portraits of the Renaissance.

The best way to explain how temporary aloofness from science could foster the growth of humanistic thought and, indirectly, even that of later science, is to refer to the role played by early humanists in the overthrow of astrological superstition. It is well known that Petrarch's fight against the Averroists of Padua sprang to a large extent from his resistance to astrology, which permeated science in the Averroist atmosphere. So closely knit were astrological notions with the fabric of all science in the late Middle Ages that Petrarch, clinging to Cicero's scorn of superstition of every type, was almost unique in rejecting astrology as a whole. Against this fourteenth-century background one must note the following facts from the Quattrocento. When in its second half leading humanists — as well as philosophers influenced by the humanist movement — began to remove the ban on science, the result was a widespread return to astrology, a century and a half after Petrarch. Giovanni Pontano at Naples then worked out what may be called a system of astrological psychology, while Marsilio Ficino in Florence contributed a type of astrological medicine — innovations in the field of science that were by no means dead-born, but ushered in a new era of astrological ascendancy which, in many respects, was to last until the middle of the seventeenth century. Now it is true that the same terminal decades of the Quattrocento saw the first systematic and conclusive attack upon astrology — the famous books of *Disputationum in Astrologiam* by Giovanni Pico della Mirandola. But this criticism did not come from the most advanced scientist, but was ventured by the very Italian thinker who kept aloof from renewed contacts with science more completely than did any of his important contemporaries. What, then, was the source of inspiration for this epoch-making exploit?

Professor Cassirer, in his presentation of the philosophy of the Renaissance, offers the following account: "The belief in the creative power and autonomy of man, this genuinely humanistic belief, was the factor to triumph over astrology with Pico," not empirical-scientific motives, not "the new methods of observation and mathematical computation." "The first decisive blow was struck before these methods reached perfection. The real motive for the liberation from astrology was not the new concept of nature, but the new concept of the intrinsic dignity of man." More recently Cassirer has added this perspective: "It is curious to consider how much harder it was for Kepler, a veritable scientific genius, to escape the bonds of the astrological way of thinking. . . . Kepler himself could probably not have taken the final step, had not Pico, upon whom he expressly relies, preceded him . . . : there was needed a new attitude and a new sense of the world." There may still be some doubt, as Cassirer himself says, as to the extent to which lay movements outside Italy — particularly the *Devotio Moderna* — contributed their religious spiritualism to the humanistic roots of Pico's critical assault, especially through the agency of Cusanus — a problem of European interchange to which we shall presently return. But the essential lesson to be learned concerning the relationship between fifteenth-century science and the cultural innovations in the Quattrocento scene is clear: the humanists were not entirely wrong in their belief that natural science in the fourteenth- and fifteenth-century phase had little to contribute to the new ideas championed by humanism.

But with this eclipse of natural science, however logical under fifteenth-century conditions, how could humanistic culture have been close in spirit to modern thought? To ask this question is, in Dr. Durand's eyes, to reveal its absurdity. Yet it is a precise parallel to the questions that we have tried to answer in the field of political history. There, in fact, we observed a structure of Quattrocento life that did in many respects foreshadow the modern pattern, despite the circumstance that certain fundamentals of the modern state (nation-wide unity and representative government) were lacking in the Italian Renaissance. These facts should warn us to withhold judgment with regard to "tradition" and "innovation" in intellectual life, until both possible perspectives — that of similarities in "structure" as well as that of "continuity" — have been discerned.

A milestone in our knowledge of the rise of science, no doubt, is the discovery that positive scientific work, gradually expanding beyond the ancient legacy, was started in the late medieval schools; that in this way a tradition was built up which was still an essential element in Galileo's day; and that fifteenth-century Italy contributed but little to this coherent growth. Yet with our knowledge of the effects of humanistic thought on astrology, we must conclude that this discovery does not settle the problem in all its aspects. It certainly does not exclude the possibility that, outside the continuity of academic science, the Quattrocento may have produced such philosophic views and intellectual habits as on the one hand could foreshadow characteristics of the later "scientific mind" and on the other in due time react on science itself. This means that the question still remains, to what extent did the general transformation of the cultural atmosphere in the Quattrocento either anticipate or even *indirectly* influence the change from "medieval" to "modern" science in the sixteenth century?

Couched in these general terms, the problem seems to threaten to lead us into that blind alley of search for an "intangible spirit," against which Dr. Durand warns us in his paper. But the vagueness disappears as soon as the inquiry is reduced to the concrete questions, how far the scientific revolution of the sixteenth century was a consequence solely of the intrinsic growth of thought, a product of the cooperative efforts of schools and academic associations; and how far, in the critical stage, even science was dependent on contemporary changes in moral values, religious and philosophical convictions, and on the relations of thought and practical experience in the life of those engaged in scientific pursuits. This problem, already attacked by recent students, is open to proof or disproof by historical evidence. Should we find essential contributions made by factors reacting on science from outside, then fifteenth-century Italy, despite its barrenness in science in the proper sense, may still appear as instrumental in producing the indispensable frame for the sixteenth-century revolution of science.

The first example to be examined in this light concerns the possible role of the "Quattrocento spirit" only in part, since the developments of lay society and thought outside Italy had a large share in its intellectual formation. But as the case of Cusanus, which I have in mind, contains the most challenging implications for every approach to fifteenth-century science, it has become a focal point for Renaissance debate and has been used as such by Dr. Durand. However, as the intellectual forces by which Cusanus mind was moulded were largely of non-Italian origin — an earlier counterpart to the mixture of northern and Italian elements in Pico della Mirandola — it should be emphasized that our characterization of the Renaissance as a "prototype" of the modern world is not meant to imply that every aspect of modern thought must first have appeared in fifteenth-century Italy. Many well-known phases of Quattrocento life undoubtedly had parallels in the contemporary culture of other European countries, and not a few characteristics of the modern mind — particularly all those connected with the rise of a new lay piety — found even more favorable conditions outside of Italy. Quattrocento culture gives the well-known illusion of a "radical break with the Middle Ages," because the peculiar structure of Italian society and its kinship with ancient Roman civilization intensified cultural change and caused so rapid a pace of evolution that fifteenth-century Italy experienced many social and intellectual developments which did not appear in the rest of Europe until centuries later. Yet, even so, the Italian Renaissance was merely part of a greater phenomenon, which, in different ways, and with varying speed, was appearing all over Europe. There was constant interrelation between the "Italian Renaissance" and the Renaissance as a movement continental in scope. The first great personality in whom all the elements of Renaissance "innovation," both inside and outside Italy, combined was Nicholas of Cusa.

Cusanus' role in the overthrow of medieval cosmology — before cosmology had become a part of Renaissance interests in Italy — has given rise to the most conflicting interpretations. Professor Durand has recalled the fact that certain German scholars made the mistake of reading "anticipations of Copernicus into the mystico-scientific speculations of Nicholas of Cusa," while they attributed heliocentric ideas to this mystic of the fifteenth century — an error that has been bitterly assailed by Thorndike. One must insist, however, that these corrections have settled the matter only so far as the time and circumstances of the emergence of modern astronomical concepts are concerned. The general historical problem in the background, the real cause of those misinterpretations, is left unsolved. The intricacy of this problem is revealed by the fact that, although Cusanus did not have at his disposal, nor did he anticipate, the relevant astronomical data, he did develop the notion that the earth was not low and vile, far below the divine heavens of the stars, but was itself a "noble star," along with the others. He rejoiced over this vindication of the earth in words that were well known to and almost literally repeated by the founders of the heliocentric theory in the sixteenth century — while even in the seventeenth century acceptance of the Copernican system was still obstructed by the argument that the earth, in consequence of her "vileness," must be in the center of the universe, this being the worst possible place and farthest removed from the incorrupti-

ble bodies of the stars. All these facts and similar aspects of the Cusanus case have been emphatically pointed out by two philosophers who can hardly be suspected of having any chauvinistic axes to grind — Professor Cassirer (in the introductory chapter of his *Individuum und Kosmos in der Renaissance*) and Professor Lovejoy (in the chapter "The Principle of Plenitude and the New Cosmology," in his *Great Chain of Being*).

From this the only plausible conclusion seems to be that in the case of cosmology the isolated study of the history of science leads one astray; that the perspective that emerged from mysticism — or, better, from a combination of mysticism, Platonism, and stimuli from the Italian Renaissance — for the evaluation of life and a metaphysical interpretation of the world, anticipated observations in astronomical science leading to similar conceptions of the universe.

But if in this case the growth of science was closely intertwined with strands of thought which had their origin outside the scientific sphere, can we believe that a profound mutation of culture and society, such as that which took place in Italy, would not have finally reacted on science in a similar way, on an even grander scale, and with more conclusive results? It is, of course, impossible to attempt any exhaustive inquiry into this problem within the compass of this critique. Moreover, the selection of evidence depends largely upon the notions of "science" that are taken as a standard — notions that are disputed and must be adapted to the changing needs of Renaissance research by experts in the history of science. Still, certain general conclusions suggest themselves immediately when for the Quattrocento such problems are raised as have been recently discussed by students of the period of Galileo.

There is no better subject to begin with than cosmology, as the discussion of Cusanus has revealed. It is not necessary to emphasize the bonds of kinship which had existed between the *Weltanschauung* of the Middle Ages and a type of cosmology which held that the heaven of the stars was composed of ether, an element purer than anything on this sinful earth; where man lifted up his eyes to the changeless movements of the stars — signs of divine perfection and eternal laws, for which he knew no parallel on earth. Not for scientific reasons alone, therefore, did the idea of the universe as a hierarchy composed of pure and less pure spheres hold the allegiance of medieval man. This cosmic system was consistent with this habit of thinking in terms of a gradational hierarchy and a static divine order in all spheres of life. When Galileo struck the final blow against this old cosmology, proving that the stars are made of stuff no different from earthly things, and that they follow the same natural laws that rule the human sphere, he rebelled against the medieval past not only as a scientist, but also as a son of an epoch in which man rejoiced in the idea that earth and stars and every particle of the universe are equal in perfection, none degraded for eternity. To regard this new frame of mind as sufficient cause for Galileo's attempt to prove the operation of the same laws in the stellar sphere and on earth, would be to overstress a single factor. But the distortion is equal when the profound change in the human evaluation of life, which was a necessary concomitant of the transition from a gradational and static to a decentralized and dynamic universe, is regarded as negligible. When Galileo jubilantly noted the definite proof that this our earth is physically one with moon and stars, *non autem sordium mundanarumque fecum sentinam esse,* he knew that he was repeating the triumphant words of Cusanus, uttered long before the claim was supported by scientific discoveries. He also knew that he was transforming and expressing in exact mathematical language the lofty idea of a decentralized, infinite Nature, evolved from philosophical speculation — first through the vitalism and panpsychism dominating biology, medicine, and chemistry early in the sixteenth century, and finally by Giordano Bruno's pantheistic conviction that one and the same divine power unfolds itself restlessly in every particle of the world.

Today, because of the prevailing tendency to accept the coming of the mathematical method as the decisive factor distinguishing "new" from "old," Giordano Bruno, who once seemed to represent the climax of Renaissance philosophy, has receded into the background. Yet Bruno, standing at the crossroads, provides the best evidence that genuine elements of the Renaissance went into the crucible of modern scientific thought. Although he failed to perceive the full meaning of the mathematical method and the mathematical concept of the infinite, he had a firm grip on the cosmological idea of the infinity of the universe, and in it found a sufficient basis for revolt against the Aristotelian-scholastic concepts of finite space and a finite world. From Bruno's work one can perceive the almost logical train of the phases of Renaissance thought: experience of the boundlessness of human passion and of the search for knowledge — the basis common to Renaissance ethics and psychology since Petrarch — found a corollary in the idea of the infinitude of the physical universe; while the infinitude of physical energies in turn needed as its vehicle, as it were, the infinitude of space — the idea that was to burst asunder the concept of a static finite world. "Here too" — quoting from Cassirer's description of this fundamental concatenation of Renaissance thought — "it is a dynamic motive which overcomes the static structure of Aristotelian-scholastic cosmology, . . . not (yet) as a new science of dynamics, but as a new dynamic feeling underlying the cosmological outlook."

In other words, the story of the birth of modern science cannot be fully told before inquiry is made into the causes of the rising tendency to see life in a "dynamic" vision; before it is explained how the belief in the universe as an immovable, God-given order was overcome by the idea of a decentralized, infinite universe, a world in evolution, and so paved the way for the later readiness to reduce all physical phenomena to a successive flux, and for the evolutionary views characteristic of modern thought.

To reconstruct this story means to find a place for the fifteenth-century Renaissance in the rise of science. The static world of medieval man had inspired conviction as long as the idea of hierarchic order had reigned supreme in every field, in human history as well as nature. The famous doctrine of four universal empires succeeding one another as a divinely created frame of history, with the Roman empire as the last, placed above historical flux and destined to endure to the end of history, was the exact equivalent in historical outlook of the gradation of the crystal spheres in the Ptolemaic system. Again, when the idea of a *Sacrum Imperium,* more "perfect" than the other states, was destroyed by the notion of a decentralized history with empires and smaller states all on one level of natural growth and decay, the revolution in historical outlook thus revealed was a precise counterpart to the emergence of a dynamic, decentralized view of nature. The intellectual and psychological effects of rebellion in either sphere were bound to be akin and to react on one another.

But the two processes, although related in their meaning for intellectual life, did not occur at the same time. At the end of the Middle Ages, as in all other periods of history, intellectual energy was first concentrated on certain sectors of life until, with revolutionary results achieved, interest shifted to other fields. By the end of the humanistic Renaissance of the Quattrocento, a dynamic, decentralized view had emerged in history and political science, with its first great expression in the works of Machiavelli and Guicciardini. In the sixteenth century the same vision began to transform cosmology and, indeed, all notions of nature. Machiavelli's *Discorsi sopra la prima deca di Tito Livio* (finished, in substance, in 1513) and Galileo's *Dialogo sopra i due massimi sistemi del mondo* (finished in 1632) were complementary phases of one historical process. Both deal with the same problem of the dynamic vision of a decentralized reality; both represent the triumph of the vernacular, and thus of closer contacts with the lay world, in their respective fields. Finally, to the question why the "discovery of man and history" should have occurred first in the Renaissance, while the "discovery of nature" followed, the answer seems to be that the experience and sentiments of the citizen of the Italian Commune first produced new conceptions of culture, politics, and history. When the historical outlook and the ideas of human nature had been remade, the change in perspective, in a second phase, would react on natural science.

If these considerations are sound, fifteenth-century Italy contributed one of the most decisive "innovations" to the development of modern science. This contribution, it is true, had little immediate effect on science, but in the broader intellectual life it caused the rise of those very problems and attitudes of mind that were to provide the indispensable frame of thought for the transition from "medieval" to "modern" science, a hundred years later. Now one may wonder whether inquiry into the nature of such general cultural relations must be included in the discussion of the evolution of natural science and should not be left rather to the care of students in other fields, particularly in the history of philosophy. However, the need for specialization in practical research is one thing, while the need to give to individual results their proper place in a synoptic vision of all the vital forces of a period is another. If it is true that mental attitudes and problems are apt to spread across the separate departments of culture, and that this dissemination of new concepts often requires the span of generations, two inferences seem inevitable: first, that no estimate of the forces of "tradition" and "innovation" in any period is reliable if based on research in a single field; and second, that neither science, nor political thought, nor any single cultural activity can be understood in its specific evolution, unless allowance is made for cases in which essentials of pro-

gressive growth — for instance, the awareness of natural laws, or the power to make
casual observation and research — are born
and first elaborated in sectors of intellectual
life remote from the particular field of our
learned specialization.

In historical sciences older and riper than
the comparatively recent Renaissance scholarship, integration of the results of study in
neighboring fields has undoubtedly pro-
gressed much farther than in present Renaissance research. A familiar example is, in
the history of early Greece, the unraveling
of the subtle threads connecting Ionic nature philosophy and the political thought
of the Sophists. It may be useful to bring
home the point by quoting the following
account from Professor Sabine's recent
History of Political Theory:

At the start the fundamental [Greek] idea
of harmony or proportionality was applied indifferently as a physical and as an ethical principle and was conceived indifferently as a
property of nature or as a reasonable property
of human nature. The first development of the
principle, however, took place in natural philosophy, and this development reacted in turn
upon its later use in ethical and political
thought. . . . The objects that made up the
physical world were to be explained on the
hypothesis that they were variations or modifications of an underlying substance which in
essence remained the same. The contrast here
is between fleeting and ever-changing particu-
lars and an unchangeable "nature" whose
properties and laws are eternal. . . . But at
about the middle of the fifth century . . . [there
was] a swing in the direction of humanistic
studies, such as grammar, music, the arts of
speech and writing, and ultimately psychology,
ethics, and politics. . . . The Greeks had [now]
become familiar . . . with the variety and the
flux of human custom. What more natural,
then, than that they should find in custom and
convention the analogue of fleeting appearances and should seek again for a "nature" or a
permanent principle by which the appearances
could be reduced to regularity? The "substance" of the physical philosophers consequently reappeared as a "law of nature," eternal amid the endless qualifications and
modifications of human circumstance.

There is no reason why, in the fifteenth
and sixteenth centuries of our era, the in-
verse sequence of, first, humanism and
politico-historical science and, secondly,
natural science should not be interpreted in
similar terms. When viewed in this light,
the balance between "promise" and "prejudice" in the Quattrocento will take on a
different aspect.

So far we have attempted to show that a
change in the structure of intellectual life
did have a part in the growth of positive
science in the sixteenth century, and that
there had been precedents in fifteenth-century Italy for the new frame of mind essential in Galileo's period. With these facts as
a background, there is more concrete meaning in the claim that the importance of the
Quattrocento lay in a new type of thinking,
in a fresh approach to intellectual problems,
and not in the extent of the innovations
that were immediately effected in the specific sciences and arts.

We may now add a second illustration —
one hardly less decisive, taken from the
sociological aspects of modern science. This
factor Dr. Durand touches upon when he
mentions "the happy union of the hand, the
eye, and the mind, which reached its perfection in Leonardo da Vinci," i.e., the observational and experimental work of Quattrocento artists and engineers outside of
humanism and academic science — a trend
unfortunately excluded from Dr. Durand's
picture because (in his own words) the
assessment of its "theoretical contributions
to the whole of Quattrocento science must
wait for further monographic research." But
are we really justified, on this ground, in
omitting an appraisal of these artist groups
from an attempted "balance sheet" of the
fifteenth-century Renaissance? If their
"fruitful work," as Dr. Durand says, was
"undeniably a chief glory of Quattrocento
Italy," it is difficult to see how one could
reach any fair balance between its elements
of tradition and innovation, while eliminat-
ing one of the most interesting potential
factors of "innovation." Fortunately for our
purposes, the point about these groups most

strongly emphasized by recent students is not so much their possible contribution of clearly defined theories, as the psychological and intellectual consequences of the appearance of foci of practical, unacademic investigation in the field of science. But before applying the sociological perspective of the fifteenth-century set-up, we must provide a framework by summarizing the results already gained with this approach for the history of science in the period of Galileo.

The import of Galileo's scientific work springs, roughly speaking, from two major achievements: his bringing to a triumphant conclusion the cosmological revolution that had been growing throughout the Renaissance; and his reduction, final and irrevocable, of science to measurement, quantity, and motion — to mathematics working on data supplied by observation, checked by experiment. To the problems of the origin of this mathematical method much study has been given in recent years. To a degree, stress of mathematics as the core of true knowledge, had long been an element of Platonist epistemology and metaphysics. In the wake of Platonism, it had come to the fore with Cusanus, and again with Kepler, a fact highly emphasized by Cassirer in his various works. Yet, though positive science — in its Averroist and its Ockhamite branches — developed at the late medieval universities, and induction, observation, and even the precedents of Galileo's combination of analytic-resolutive and constructive-compositive methods gradually appeared, mathematics did not, until the middle of the sixteenth century, obtain its modern place in scientific research. In the School of Padua — as shown by Professor Randall and re-emphasized by Professor Durand — it was largely from the Latin revisions of Archimedes by Tartaglia in 1543 and by Commandino in 1558, that mathematical interests and methods slowly began to penetrate physical science.

These conclusions, important and definite though they are, seem to require some comment. The appearance of a convenient revised edition of the familiar work of an ancient mathematician, however eagerly welcomed and utilized by leading Paduan scholars, would not in itself explain the triumph of the mathematical method. The publication and its effects are remarkable rather as a straw in the wind, because they signalize a trend of interest which was developing in the second half of the sixteenth century. The origin of Tartaglia's interest in mathematics had little to do with the science of Padua or with any of the older schools. Tartaglia was a self-taught man, who had made all his discoveries in mathematics and mechanics in intercourse with practical engineers, gunners, merchants, and architects in northern Italy. A few decades later there were similar conditions affecting the development of Galileo. In his youth, unable to find an opportunity for mathematical training in the University of Pisa, Galileo acquired the mathematical interest characteristic of his later work by making contacts with the same type of practical mathematics. His studies were pursued under a teacher who belonged to the *Accademia del Disegno* in Florence, a kind of technical institute for the preparation of artists, architects, and engineers.

Thus the conclusion is suggested that it was contact with experimenting, practically-minded technicians and masters outside the schools that infused the decisive element, a fresh compound of experiment and mathematics, into late medieval science. It is this point that serves as a *leit-motiv* in the monograph on *Galilei und seine Zeit* published by Professor Olschki in 1927 — a work which first called full attention to the connection of Tartaglia and Galileo with the mathematical pursuits of artists, architects, and engineers outside the academic circles. More recently, studies by Dr. Edgar Zilsel, still in progress, have traced the early contacts of the academic world with the new class of workshop engineers and foremen in the countries outside Italy — particularly from the middle of the sixteenth century onward, when scholars first undertook observational studies in the mines and foundries of the new capitalistic industries. There may be some danger of exaggeration in Zilsel's claim that the "decisive event in the genesis of science" about 1600 lay in the uniting of the two previously separated groups — the educated, theoretically-minded "upper stratum," and the practical work-men in the shops and mines, the "lower stratum," which "added causal spirit, experi-mentation, measurement, quantitative rules of operation, disregard of school authority, and objective co-operation." Yet there is one outstanding fact which may be definitively inferred from Olschki's and Zilsel's find-ings: it is now better understood why natu-ral science in the modern sense depended on the rise of a new society, no less than did humanistic education and the new po-litical and historical sciences. The point in common is that the emergence of a new phase was everywhere bound up with the appearance of lay circles living a life of work and action from which evolved new practical skills and subsequently new theories, ideas, and evaluations of life. What the rise of an urban society, com-posed of practical men participating as readers and writers in a type of literature no longer produced for one rank only, meant for humanist education; what the reappearance of active political citizenship in the Italian city-states meant for political studies: this the emergence of groups edu-cated and engaged in technological pursuits meant for the beginnings of the new natu-ral science.

Viewed in this light the Quattrocento reveals itself once more as a prototype of the modern pattern — as a precursor, even if on a somewhat variant basis. It is true that the high tide for the new technical classes, as Zilsel emphasizes, did not come until the full rise of capitalism in the min-ing, metal and related industries in the six-teenth century, while fifteenth-century Italy clung to the "ancient distinction be-tween liberal and mechanical arts," with the one exception of painters and sculptors, who were "gradually detached from handi-craft and slowly rose to social esteem." But it was in fact this exception which in the Quattrocento brought about the first con-tacts of any practical profession with scien-tific theory, awakening scientific interest in a general cultured public outside human-ism and the academic schools. In the con-ditions of Renaissance Italy the workshop of the artist, in fostering experimental work and stimulating observation and causal thinking, performed precisely the intellec-tual function that was in later centuries discharged by the industrial workshop and the scientific laboratory.

There were in the art of the Renaissance several elements capable of promoting this effect. To begin with, a type of art that placed proportion first, made truth to nature an indispensable standard, and included in the work of the artist-architect town-plan-ning and the technique of fortifications, was bound to promote mathematical and experimental methods far beyond the reach of the medieval Schoolmen. Moreover, it was in the heart of the new urban society that the new technical skills were practiced. While passing from the detached, collectiv-ist orbit of the masons' gild engaged in the construction and adornment of a medieval church, to the workshop of the "artist-engi-neer" in a busy Florentine street, art had in fact travelled a distance equivalent to that covered in the intellectual transition from the clerical atmosphere of medieval monas-teries and universities to the symbiosis of thought and action in the society of the Renaissance. Thanks to the pioneering work of Professors Olschki and Julius von Schlosser we are able to form a very clear idea of those early counting, measuring, experimenting masters, accustomed to pur-sue self-taught studies in optics, perspective, anatomy, and the engineering work con-nected with the great architectural projects of the Renaissance. From Florentine groups which included Ghiberti, Brunelleschi, L. B. Alberti, and Filarete, there extended a coherent tradition of skills and interests down to circles subsequently formed at the courts of Urbino and Milan, with the climax in the great figure of Leonardo. Continued throughout the sixteenth century, this trend became an essential influence (as was said above) on Galileo in his youth.

For Florence our documents permit us to observe the existence of constant and intimate contacts between the most diversified groups of citizens, including the humanist literati, and masters of this type working on technical as well as artistic projects. The universal curiosity aroused by the public competition of Florentine artists for the adornment of the doors of the Baptistry in 1401 is mentioned in every history of the Renaissance, and the emotional appeal to the Florentine public of the pioneering problems involved in the construction of the cathedral dome strikingly foreshadowed the general interest in great technical feats in later centuries. Professor Krey, in a recent pamphlet, has given a convincing account of the importance and intensity of this exchange between the craftsman and the cultured citizen, the artist and the humanist. That early humanists did not include scientific studies in their program should therefore not cause us to forget this subtle education of Renaissance society in scientific interests and ways of thought. There was a growing effect on intellectual life and even on humanism in the second half of the Quattrocento. If it did not produce originality in the field of natural science, it still reacted on the literary production of the mature Renaissance, providing writers with a scientific background which aided them in finding realistic ways of thought in many fields of literature and learning. In the Florence of Lorenzo de' Medici the Neo-Platonists as well as humanists of the type of Poliziano were all in intercourse with Toscanelli's circle, and the effects are palpable in their work. As to Machiavelli, his dependence on medical and biological ideas was demonstrated by O. Tammasini in his huge monograph thirty years ago. Had scientific pursuits as yet not played a part, side by side with classical and political interests, in the Florentine groups which influenced the growth of Machiavelli's thought, he would hardly have possessed the intellectual tools he needed for his naturalistic analysis of political disintegration and growth.

All these factors throw light upon the existence of subtle interrelations between the "realism" of the Renaissance and the subsequent rise of the scientific spirit. But it is necessary to turn to the lonely, gigantic figure of Leonardo da Vinci to realize fully the promise for the future inherent in the scientific by-ways of the Quattrocento. Whatever may be the final verdict upon the thesis offered by Duhem — i.e., that Leonardo as a scientist largely exploited the work of Scholastic predecessors — it is evident even today that by the artist of the Renaissance something substantial was added to the legacy of the Schoolmen — a new achievement springing from the milieu of the artist-engineers of the Quattrocento. This addition was not only an advance in practical experimental skills; it included the very element which was to become the mark of modern science — the ascendancy of the mathematical method. Leonardo, long before mathematics became the royal road of academic science, contended unambiguously that "no human investigation can be called true science without passing through mathematical tests." He was convinced that any step beyond this solid foundation would lead to the illusion of understanding the substance of things, a knowledge of which "the human mind is incapable." And in place of the old hierarchy of sciences, with metaphysics and theology supreme, he first envisaged a gradation of studies in terms of the certitude they derived from the degree in which they were penetrated by mathematics.

This sudden and unique anticipation of the method of modern science is, of course, more than an isolated fact. It points to a substantial affinity between Leonardo's vision of nature and the modern scientific outlook. Indeed, viewed from any angle of the great transition from a static-centralized to a dynamic-evolutionary view of life, Leonardo's ideas and discoveries herald the things to come. With him Cusanus' exulta-

tion over the earth as one with the other
stars — the "glory of our universe," as
Leonardo said with Cusanus — led to the
first dynamic interpretation, not only of
the cosmos, but of nature as a whole. To
Leonardo, in the geological history of the
earth, the Deluge had ceased to be the all-
determining event — a counterpart to the
eclipse of the *Sacrum Imperium* in historical thought — giving way to a vision of incessant flux and change. For the first time
the geological scene of human life appeared
as the work of oceans, rivers, winds, a world
in which plants, animals, and men grow in
a natural way — until this planet in some
distant future shall have become cold and
dry, by the workings of the same natural
forces, in the same natural cycle of growth
and decay. It is the keenness of his per-
ception of the dynamic rotation of nature
from destruction to reproduction that led
Leonardo to many of his startling discoveries — such as his understanding of the
change of species in flora and fauna in the
course of geological history, and of the incessant processes of consumption and reproduction in all living substance. For an
historical perspective of the Renaissance
the most important point is not the fact
that these discoveries along with many of
Leonardo's technological inventions foreshadowed some of the later attainments of
science in an astounding way, but that in
their entirety they revealed the same dynamic vision contemporaneously at work in
the remaking of political and historical science by Machiavelli —the vision of reality
that was to transmute cosmology and, subsequently, all positive sciences, from the
second half of the sixteenth century onward. One may attempt to indicate Galileo's place in intellectual history with the
three key-words of experimental observation, mathematical method, and the dynamic view of a decentralized nature. All
these basic avenues of the later science
Quattrocento thought had entered a
century before, and in no half-hearted
fashion.

With this delineation of the historical
role of the "artist-engineer" we are in a position to appraise, in a fresh and concrete
way, the meaning of the claim that a new
type of man and thought appeared with the
Quattrocento. The older interpretations of
the Renaissance, based on fifteenth-century
humanism and the political conditions of
the Quattrocento, have been repeated and
confirmed in the investigation of a new
sector of Quattrocento life. Wherever, we
may say, creative individuals belonged to
social groups which had direct contacts
with the new life of work and action —
whether we think of the official-secretary, or
the merchant-statesman, or the artist-engi-
neer — there the transformed relationship
of life and thought rapidly gave to experience, interests, and accepted values the
shape that differentiates the modern from
the medieval mind.

In the perspective of present-day research, the upshot then seems to be that
Burckhardt's analysis of the Renaissance as
a new phase of psychological and intellectual development still holds its own. The
definition and formulation of the results
attainable through his approach have been,
no doubt, modified and re-modified in the
course of eighty years of subsequent investigation. What in Burckhardt's day appeared
as one perspective, is now refracted in divergent strains of thought. Most of the
students who still follow Burckhardt as a
guide feel that his dictum of "the discovery
of the world and of man" in the Italian
Renaissance, i.e., his characterization of the
period as that of the triumph of "realism"
and "individualism," is in the light of the
concrete problems of present scholarship incomplete, and needs specification. One
group of recent students has emphasized
the place of the Renaissance in what we
have described as the transition from a
static-gradational and centralized idea of
life and the world to a dynamic-evolutionary and decentralized concept of man, history, and nature. Others, under the impact
of increasing evidence that there was much
of realism in medieval thought and art, feel
it imperative to redefine the "realism" of

the Renaissance — a redefinition which shifts the emphasis to the fifteenth-century discovery of objective laws in nature, history, and human psychology, with the laws of mathematics in a place of special significance for the rise of science. In the last analysis these varied views are not alternative, but complementary to each other. They represent the different avenues along which recent scholarship has been developing the Burckhardtian thesis that at the basis of the fifteenth-century Renaissance there was a fundamental change in man's outlook on life and the world — the coming of the "first-born among the sons of modern Europe."

If, on the other hand, we are today more aware than Burckhardt of the immense importance of the continuity binding the ideas and institutions of the modern world to the medieval past, this insight neither needs nor has the power to undo the lesson learned from a century of studies of the Italian Renaissance. The task before us is increasingly to integrate the two great vistas opened up by medieval and Renaissance research, neither of which gains by their mutual disparagement.

THE PLACE OF CLASSICAL HUMANISM
IN RENAISSANCE THOUGHT

PAUL OSKAR KRISTELLER

Paul Oskar Kristeller, Professor of Philosophy at Columbia University, was born and educated in Germany. His research and many publications reveal a wide and profound knowledge of Renaissance thought and its classical background. Much of his attention has been centered on the person of Marsilio Ficino as the outstanding Platonist in the intellectual and philosophical history of the Italian Renaissance. Professor Kristeller is also widely known as a special lecturer and visiting professor both here and abroad.

THE "problem of the Renaissance," as it has been widely discussed in the last few decades, is largely a pseudo-problem. A complex historical period with a great variety of cross-currents, in which each European country and each field of interest underwent its own particular development, can hardly be interpreted in terms of a brief definition which would at the same time distinguish it from all other periods of history. Such definitions are apt to be too narrow or too broad. The discussion has been further complicated by the tendency of many scholars to take the Renaissance as an imaginary battle-ground on which to fight out contemporary political, social and ideological conflicts, or as a test case for the solution of such metahistorical questions as

From P. O. Kristeller, "The Place of Classical Humanism in Renaissance Thought," in the *Journal of the History of Ideas,* IV (1943), 59–63. By permission of the editors of the *Journal of the History of Ideas.*

the possibility and the causes of historical change. On the other hand, there seems no doubt about the distinctive physiognomy of the Renaissance, and the claim that the very existence of "the Renaissance" has to be proved by a satisfactory definition of it, must be rejected. With the same right, we might as well conclude that there was no "eighteenth century," since we are unable to describe its distinctive characteristics in a brief definition. The best procedure would be rather to start with a tentative conception of the Renaissance, and to take this idea as a guiding principle when investigating the actual facts and sources of the period under consideration.

The question which Professor Durand sets out to answer is much more specific: what is the contribution of fifteenth-century Italy to the progress of natural science? I think the question is worth asking, and we must be grateful for the judicious way in which he has presented and evaluated the facts discovered through recent studies in the history of science. He rightly emphasizes the continuity of the university tradition, and at the same time recognizes the importance of the new translations from the Greek, as in the case of Ptolemy's *Geography*. Many other scientific translations, commentaries, and treatises of the fifteenth century are still awaiting a more detailed investigation, and many other branches of science and learning will have to be examined. But most probably Professor Durand's conclusion will be confirmed, that fifteenth-century Italy brought no basic change in the methods and results of natural science, although it contributed numerous observations and theories in the various fields.

I disagree, however, with the conclusions for the general interpretation of the Renaissance Professor Durand seems to draw from this result. I fully agree with Professor Baron's excellent definition of the relation between the history of science and intellectual history in general, and his emphasis on the powerful influence with important changes in other fields eventually exercised on the development of natural science. The question of tradition and innovation in Renaissance science cannot be definitely settled without taking into consideration the non-professional writers on science, the non-Italian scientists, many of whom were more or less indebted to the Italians, and possibly even the scientists of the sixteenth century who largely reaped what the fifteenth century had sown. Moreover, science has not always occupied that dominating place among the other fields of culture which it has held during the last few centuries of occidental history. We cannot accept the claim that historical changes are unimportant unless they are changes in the field of science or immediately affect science. In the case of the Renaissance, the cultural change did not primarily concern science. Since Burckhardt's conception of the Renaissance is not based on any claim for a basic change in natural science, I do not see how it can be disproved by showing that actually no such basic change in science took place. On the other hand, I agree with Professor Baron that a change did take place in fields other than science, and that this change did influence the development of science, though indirectly and in a later period.

But when I try to answer the question, what kind of change was characteristic of the Renaissance, and especially of fifteenth-century Italy, I find myself less in agreement with Professor Baron than with Professor Durand. I do believe that classical humanism was, if not the only, certainly the most characteristic and pervasive intellectual current of that period. With its merits and with its limitations, humanism pervaded more or less all achievements and expressions of the fifteenth century. When its influence declined in the sixteenth century, its work had been already done. The influence of humanism on science as well as on philosophy was indirect, but powerful. The actual performance of the humanists in these fields was rather poor. But they popularized the entire body of ancient Greek learning and literature and thus made available new source materials of which the professional scientists and philosophers could not fail to take advantage. This was important, because at that time occidental science and thought had not yet reached or surpassed the results of classical antiquity, and hence had still something to learn from the ancients. Moreover, medieval science had developed in definite patterns, and the introduction of new sources and "authorities" eventually prepared the way for new methods and theories. Those who claim that ancient science was completely known to the Middle Ages are as mistaken as those who deny that it was known at all. At least some of the classical Latin authors became more widely known in the Renaissance, Lucretius, for example. Numerous Greek manuscripts were brought over from the East, and more men were able to read them in the original. Moreover, practically all the Greek texts were translated into Latin by the humanists, many for the first time. The question of how many were translated for the first time and whether the new translations were better or more influential than the extant earlier translations, cannot be settled by dispute, but only by a careful bibliography of the Latin translations from the Greek, which should include the manuscript materials. In the field of philosophy, humanism introduced most of the works of Plato, Plotinus, Epictetus, Diogenes Laertius, Plutarch, Lucian, as well as many works of the commentators on Aristotle and of the Greek Fathers, not to speak of the Greek poets, historians, and orators. In science the contribution may be less impressive, but it has still to be investigated. Archimedes and Hero came at least to be more widely known, and many of the minor mathematicians were translated for the first time. The Latin translations were followed by extensive commentaries, and by translations into the various vernacular languages which reached an ever wider public.

The humanists were certainly not the only representatives of science and learning in the fifteenth century. On the one hand, there were the followers of the medieval traditions who carried on the work of their predecessors, especially at the various universities. On the other hand, there were the artists and engineers who through their practical work came face to face with mathematical and scientific problems and sometimes made important contributions, as has been recently emphasized. But in the fifteenth century both of these latter groups were influenced by humanism, as was the general public. If the humanists failed to make substantial contributions to the various fields of traditional learning, they did introduce source materials and problems which could be applied to those fields. By the end of the fifteenth century, humanism had not indeed replaced the traditional learning, but the representatives of traditional learning had absorbed the achievements of humanism. This accounts for the changes and progresses which took place in the sixteenth century – just as the achievements of the artists and engineers were taken over by the professional scientists after the middle of that century. On the other hand, even the artists and engineers were subject to the influence of humanism, as Professor Baron rightly emphasizes. The personal relations between the humanists and the artists need further investigation, especially as they appear from numerous letters and poems of the humanists which have not yet been utilized for this purpose. The number of artists and engineers who made active contributions to science was still comparatively small in the fifteenth century as compared with the sixteenth. But the case of Leon Battista Alberti shows that this scientific activity of the artists cannot be separated from, or opposed to, contemporary humanism.

I cannot agree with those who identify these artists with the general public of the unlearned or who make a sharp contrast between the "Academic" humanists who wrote in Latin, and the "popular" writers who used the vernacular language. Those artists who also wrote scientific treatises certainly had some learning beyond that of the general public, and drew something from the professional learning of their time, whether it was in the medieval or in the humanistic tradition. The humanists themselves, no less than these artists, impressed the popular imagination of their time, as many anecdotes show. Since this was a matter of fashion, no real understanding on the part of the public was required. If today many admire the achievements of modern science without understanding its methods, we may well grant that in the early renaissance many admired the humanists without understanding their Latin. Moreover, the question of language is less important for our problem than might be supposed. In the fifteenth century there is abundant evidence for the mutual influence between vernacular and Neo-latin literature, and when the vernacular definitely won out in the sixteenth century, it had already absorbed the characteristic achievements of humanism, in style, terminology, literary form, and subject matter. Otherwise, it could not have replaced Latin.

To conclude, I should like to add to the statements of Professors Durand and Baron that by popularizing in the fifteenth century the works of classical antiquity, the humanists made an important, though indirect contribution to the development of science and philosophy, and that this contribution bore fruit not only in the work of the humanists themselves, but also in that of the professional scientists and artists of their time and of the following century. All these statements, however, are tentative rather than final, and subject to further revision. The only thing that really counts in Renaissance studies is the actual investigation of the extensive source materials which have not yet been included in any extant synthesis. This investigation must proceed with the cooperation of all scholars interested in the period, regardless of their point of view. In this study we should try to eliminate so far as possible our personal preference for or against this or that nation, language, class, current, or field, and to arrive at a fair evaluation of the contribution each of them has made to the whole of occidental civilization. Such an evaluation will not depend wholly on the influence, direct or distant, which each phenomenon has exercised on later developments, but will also acknowledge the inherent, "absolute" significance of many ideas and achievements which for some reason or other failed to have any visible influence. It is this significance, rather than any incidental sequence of changes or influences, which in my opinion should be the ultimate purpose of the history of ideas, if not of all history.

RENAISSANCE OR PRENAISSANCE?

LYNN THORNDIKE

Lynn Thorndike, widely known as a distinguished teacher and author, is now Professor Emeritus of History at Columbia University. His many books and articles reveal a vast knowledge of the Middle Ages and especially of medieval science. He was a founding fellow of the Mediaeval Academy of America and of L'Académie Internationale d'Histoire des Sciences, and he has served as president of the History of Science Society (1929) and as president of the American Historical Association (1955).

PROFESSOR Dana B. Durand has accused me of harbouring a personal antipathy to the Renaissance. Whether my motive is personal or rational, objective or subjective, conscious or subconscious, it must be confessed that my aversion to the term in question is even more sweeping than Durand perhaps thinks and extends to such catchwords as the Carolingian Renaissance and the twelfth-century renaissance, as well as to the more often mentioned Italian Renaissance of the fifteenth century or somewhere thereabouts. Religion may have its resurrections and revivals, but I have even less faith than Nicodemus in rebirths or restorations of whole periods of human history. I take my stand with the blind writer of Christian hymns, Fanny Crosby, who sang,

But the bird with the broken pinion never soared so high again;

with William Muldoon who said of former heavy-weight champions,

They never come back;

with Omar Khayyam who mused,

The moving finger writes and having writ
Moves on; nor all your piety nor wit

May lure it back to cancel half a line
Nor all your tears wipe out one word of it;

and with a verse from the light opera, Tom Jones,

Time is not a necromancer;
Time's a thief and nothing more.

Legacies from the past? Yes. Inheritances from previous periods? Yes. Survivals? Yes. Resemblances to our forebears? Yes. Reformations? Perhaps. Reactions? Unfortunately. But no rebirths and no restorations!

Books and works of art are about all that remains to us of the past. The latter are all too soon sadly altered, and their restoration, whether by some German professor or by a Thorwaldsen or Viollet-le-Duc, only makes them less like what they originally were. Books remain less changed by the lapse of time, but even their text may become corrupt, or the meaning of the very words they use alter in the interim. The humanists of the so-called Italian Renaissance had only a bookish knowledge of antiquity; they failed almost as dismally as have Mussolini and his Fascists to make the reality of ancient Rome live again. If, even in our own day, all the resources of the art of history aided by archaeology can give us only a

From Lynn Thorndike, "Renaissance or Prenaissance?" in the *Journal of the History of Ideas*, IV (1943), 65–74. By permission of the editors of the *Journal of the History of Ideas*. The documentation of the original article has been omitted.

faint and imperfect idea of the past, how can we expect actual renaissances of it or recognize them as such, if they were to occur? At the age of sixty I am perhaps more like myself at the age of twenty than I am like anyone else. But I couldn't possibly put myself back into the frame of mind that I had then. I have a dim recollection of it; my present state of mind is an outgrowth of it; that is all. A girl of eighteen, dressed up in the clothes which her grandmother wore when a girl of eighteen, may look more like her grandmother as she was then than her grandmother herself does now. But she will not feel or act as her grandmother felt and acted half a century or more ago. Much more tenuous is the connection between distant historical periods, and much less likely is it that historians can successfully venture upon glittering generalities about them. Who can evoke from the past more than a wraith, a phantasy, a specter, which murmurs, like the ghost in *Hamlet,* "Historian, remember me!"

It is true that history offers examples of human customs which somewhat resemble the conception of a renaissance. For instance, at Tonalamatl in ancient Mexico the recurrence of the year date 2. acatl every 52 years was considered a critical occasion, it being feared that the sun might fail to rise next day and that the evil spirits might destroy the world and mankind. Accordingly, a festival of ceremonial fire-making was held. All the old fires were carefully extinguished and at midnight on the mountain top the high-priest by rubbing sticks together kindled a new fire on the breast of a prisoner who was forthwith sacrificed. The new fire was then distributed to the temples of the surrounding cities and thence to the adjacent peoples. Old garments were thrown away and household dishes and utensils were broken or freshly painted over in token of the new lease of life given to mankind. But this rekindling and renewal was immediate, continuous, and perfunctory. Only a part of one night intervened between the two periods, not

centuries of dark ages. There was no intellectual or spiritual rebirth.

We might also adduce the influence upon our notions of revolutions and periods in history of the astrological theory of conjunctions and revolutions of the planets.

But let us turn to the development of the concept of an Italian Renaissance and begin with the translation into Latin of Ptolemy's *Geography* in the first decade of the fifteenth century. Durand is inclined to censure the previous medieval translators for neglecting this work. If they did — for a previous translation may have escaped our notice — it is to be remembered that after all the text in question consists largely of lists of ancient place-names, many of which cannot be identified and located with any assurance and are of purely historical and linguistic interest. Moreover, Ptolemy had made the Mediterranean Sea too short by one-third, whereas one of the medieval *portolani* is more accurate than any other map of the Mediterranean until the eighteenth century. Concerning the Far East, too, and islands in the Atlantic the thirteenth and fourteenth centuries were much better informed than Ptolemy. The translation and subsequent vogue of his *Geography* were therefore in some ways regrettable. Be that as it may, in the dedication of his translation to pope Alexander V, Jacobus Angelus, who was a booster of his native town of Florence, says:

This very age of ours, especially in our city of Florence, has sparkled with how many wits, who to their great glory have resuscitated liberal studies which had grown almost torpid.

In the fifth volume of *A History of Magic and Experimental Science* I have given various examples of this notion of a resuscitation of liberal studies becoming stereotyped and being extended to most inappropriate fields, such as astronomy by Moravus and Santritter, chiromancy and physiognomy by Cocles, anatomy by Vesalius, and magic in the case of Antiochus Tibertus. Abstemius depicted pope Paul III as restoring astrology after it had lain in darkness, disrepute, barbarism and sordid squalor for many centuries past; Pena praised Charles, cardinal of Lorraine, for having resuscitated the prostrate mathematical sciences. Just as the humanists who found manuscripts of the Latin classics in monasteries represented themselves as discovering the work in question and rescuing it from neglect and decay, saying nothing of the fact that the monks had copied it in Carolingian times and preserved it ever since, but leaving their own manuscripts when they died to some monastery as the safest place in which to keep them, so publishers who printed a text for the first time, even if it was a typical product of medieval scholasticism, represented themselves as snatching it from Gothic filth and dust and mildew and cobwebs and bringing it to the light of fairest impressions with the text carefully restored to its pristine purity and freed from barbarisms, when in reality they were very likely using a single inferior manuscript and neglecting a dozen older and superior versions.

When was the word, Renaissance, first used? Nicolaus Prucknerus or Prugner approached such usage when, in the preface to his re-edition of the ancient Roman astrologer, Julius Firmicus Maternus, addressed from Strasbourg on January 28, 1551, to young king Edward VI of England, he spoke of religion reviving in that realm (*una cum renascente religione istius regni*). But evidently he was speaking of the Protestant Reformation. Two years later, however, the French naturalist, Pierre Belon, in the dedicatory epistle of his *Les observations . . . de plusieurs singularitez* to François cardinal Tournon, assured him that, as a result of his patronage of learning and education of promising young scholars, it had followed that the minds of men, which were formerly as it were asleep and sunk in a profound slumber of long-standing ignorance, had begun to awake, to come forth from the shadows where they had so long dwelt, and to develop in all sorts of good disciplines a happy and desirable Renaissance, like plants that, after the rigors of

winter, regain their strength with the sun and sweetness of springtime.

Peter Ramus, in an oration delivered in 1546, made the following vivid contrast between his own and the preceding century. Suppose, he said, a master of a century ago should return to life now, what progress he would discover, how astounded he would be! He would be as surprised as one who, risen from depths of earth, should see for the first time sun, moon and stars shining bright. For then he heard no one speak except in a barbarous and inept manner, while now he would hear countless persons of every age speaking and writing Latin correctly and ornately. Then no one could read Greek, now men not only read it but understand it thoroughly. He used to hear as grammarians, poets and orators, Alexander of Villa-Dei, Facetus, the *Graecismus*; in philosophy, Scotists and followers of Petrus Hispanus; in medicine, the Arabs; in theology, I know not what upstarts. Now he would hear Terence, Caesar, Virgil, Cicero, Aristotle, Plato, Galen, Hippocrates, Moses and the prophets, the Apostles and other true and genuine messengers of the Gospel, and indeed voices in all languages.

Except for the closing allusions to vernacular translations of the Bible, this passage well expresses the original restricted significance of the Renaissance as a purification of Latin diction and grammar, a revival of Greek, and a return from medieval compilers, commentators and originators to the old classical texts. This was all that the revival of learning meant to the Italian humanists of the quattrocento and to their fellows beyond the Alps, and for them it was enough. The mere thought of it aroused in Ramus a grand and glorious feeling of enthusiasm tempered with complacency. He neither sensed any change in the political and economic set-up nor was aware of any alteration in social and moral values.

As the study and reading of Latin and Greek waned, however — and this was partly because the humanists and classicists had substituted a dead for a living language — fewer and fewer persons could sincerely share in this thrill or impart it to others. Such fervor as the concept of the Renaissance still invoked was largely in the realm of the fine arts, where the term had been applied to the post-Gothic period. It was at this juncture that Michelet called the Renaissance "the discovery of the world and of man," and was followed in this lead by the very influential book of Burckhardt, in which, on what seem too often to be dogmatic or imaginery grounds without sufficient presentation of facts as evidence, the Renaissance was no longer regarded as primarily a rebirth of classical learning and culture but rather as a prebirth or precursor of present society and of modern civilization — "a period," to quote the *Boston Transcript* (February 27, 1926) concerning Elizabethan England, "that witnessed the birth pangs of most that is worth while in modern civilization and government."

This made a well-calculated appeal to the average reader who is little interested to be told that Erasmus was a great Greek scholar or that Leonardo da Vinci copied from Albert of Saxony, but whose ego is titillated to be told that Leonardo was an individual like himself or that Erasmus's chief claim to fame is that he was the first modern man — the first one like you and me. All this was quite soothing and flattering and did much to compensate for one's inability to read Horace or to quote Euripides. It even had its appeal for professors of modern European history and for teachers of the modern languages. It appears to be the concept of the Renaissance which such recent advocates thereof or apologists therefor as Wallace K. Ferguson and Hans Baron are concerned to defend, retreating to new standing ground by plausible hypothesis and ingenious conjecture, when some of Burckhardt's old bulwarks are proved to be untenable by new masses of facts concerning either or both the middle ages and the quattrocento. But would it not make things clearer, if they ceased to employ the old name, since the old concept has been abandoned, and, instead of talking of the Renaissance, spoke of the period or movement or whatever it is they have in mind as the Prenaissance?

With regard to the work of Burckhardt I may perhaps be permitted a few further comments. Of its six parts, the third on the Revival of Antiquity seems to me scholarly and just, recognizing the defects as well as the merits of the Italian humanists and containing many bits of illuminating detail. But most of the political, social, moral and religious phenomena which he pictures as Renaissance seem almost equally characteristic of Italy at any time from the twelfth to the eighteenth century inclusive. The fourth part on the discovery of the world and man uses only popular, not scientific literature, nor may this be dismissed as merely a sin of omission, since elsewhere in the volume are such atrocious misstatements as that few works of Aristotle had been translated into Latin by the fourteenth century. By including such personalities as Frederick II and such authors and literary composition as Dante and the *Carmina burana* within the Renaissance, Burckhardt freed the movement from the embarrassment of chronological limits and made any differentiation between it and medieval culture well-nigh impossible. At bottom this was a wholesome tendency, equivalent to recognition that there is no dividing line between "medieval" and "renaissance" culture, just as most historical museums have a single section labeled "Middle Ages and Renaissance." In general, Burckhardt devoted so much of his pages and energy to the attempt to trace intangibles, such as personality, imagination, passion, spirit, the popular mind, the feeling for this and that, such and such a sentiment, that his book hardly touches the domain of intellectual history and seems to possess a will-o'-the-wisp sort of character.

The attraction which this kind of writing has for many has been well expressed by Professor Schevill in reviewing another book:

If the modern scientific method, a well co-ordinated plan, and the view-point regarding the character of the social process which obtains among present-day scholars are the indispensable requirements of a good history, it would have to be conceded that Mrs. Taylor's book stands self-condemned. But if there is salvation outside the ruling formulas, if a work may still be history, and good history, when, instead of building up a solid edifice of fact, it occupies itself with the spirit behind the facts in the hope of communicating the color and perfume of a segment of human experience, this book can be confidently recommended not only to the notoriously unscientific lovers of the Renaissance but to those grave and reverend signors, the professional historians themselves.

The trouble is that this kind of writing is almost invariably based upon an insufficient acquaintance with the facts and misinterpretation of them. Of the same genus is another bête-noire of mine, those writers who proclaim that this or that person was far in advance of his time, like Roger Bacon or Leonardo da Vinci. But should you ask them to name a few contemporaries of the person in question who were typical of that time, they would hardly be able to do so.

Was the individual freed and personality enhanced by the Renaissance or Prenaissance? Burckhardt affirmed that with it "man became a spiritual individual and recognized himself as such," whereas "in the middle ages both sides of human consciousness — that which was turned within as that which was turned without — lay dreaming or half awake beneath a common veil." It might be remarked that individualism may be a mark of decline rather than progress. The self-centred sage of the Stoics and Epicureans rang the knell of the Greek city-state. Basil, on the verge of the barbarian invasions, complained that men "for the greater part prefer individual and private life to the union of common life." Carl Neumann held that "true modern individualism has its roots in the strength of the barbarians, in the realism of the barbarians, and in the Christian middle ages." Cunningham believed that the Roman Empire "left little scope for individual aims and tended to check the energy of capitalists and laborers alike," whereas Christianity taught the supreme dignity of man and encouraged the individual and personal responsibility. Moreover, in the thirteenth century there were "fewer barriers to social intercourse than now." According to Schäfer, "So far as public life in the broadest sense, in church and state, city and country, law and society, is concerned, the middle ages are the time of most distinctive individuality and independent personality in volition and action." We may no longer think of the Gothic architects as anonymous, and de Mely discovered hundreds of signatures of miniaturists hidden in the initials and illuminations of medieval manuscripts. No period in the history of philosophy has discussed individuality and its problems more often or more subtly than did the medieval schoolmen. Vittorino da Feltre and other humanist educators may have suited their teaching to the individual pupil; at the medieval university the individual scholar suited himself. The humanists were imitative in their writing, not original. Vitruvius was the Bible of Renaissance architects who came to follow authority far more than their creative Gothic predecessors. For the middle ages loved variety; the Renaissance, uniformity.

Not only has it been demonstrated that the thirteenth and fourteenth centuries were more active and penetrating in natural science than was the quattrocento, but the notion that "appreciation of natural beauty" was "introduced into modern Europe by the Italian Renaissance" must also be abandoned. Burckhardt admitted that medieval literature displayed sympathy with nature, but nevertheless regarded Petrarch's ascent of Mount Ventoux (which is only 6260 feet high) in 1336 as epoch-making. Petrarch represented an old herdsman who had tried in vain to climb it fifty years before as beseeching him to turn back on the ground that he had received only torn clothes and broken bones for his pains and that no one had attempted the ascent since. As a matter of fact, Jean Buridan, the Parisian schoolman, had visited it between 1316 and 1334, had given details as to its altitude, and had waxed enthusiastic as to the Cevennes. So that all Petrarch's account proves is his capacity for story-telling and sentimental ability to make a mountain out of a molehill. Miss Stockmayer, in a book on feeling for nature in Germany in the tenth and eleventh centuries, has noted various ascents and descriptions of mountains from that period. In the closing years of his life archbishop Anno of Cologne climbed his beloved mountain oftener than usual.

As for the feeling for nature in medieval art, let me repeat what I have written elsewhere anent the interest displayed by the students of Albertus Magnus in particular herbs and trees.

This healthy interest in nature and commendable curiosity concerning real things was not confined to Albert's students nor to "rustic intelligences." One has only to examine the sculpture of the great thirteenth-century cathedrals to see that the craftsmen of the towns were close observers of the world of nature, and that every artist was a naturalist too. In the foliage that twines about the capitals of the columns in the French Gothic cathedrals it is easy to recognize, says M. Mâle, a large number of plants: "the plantain, arum, renunculus, fern, clover, coladine, hepatica, columbine, cress, parsley, strawberry-plant, ivy, snapdragon, the flower of the broom, and the leaf of the oak, a typically French collection of flowers loved from childhood." Mutatis mutandis, the same statement could be made concerning the carved vegetation that runs riot in Lincoln cathedral. "The thirteenth-century sculptors sang their chant de mai. All the spring delights of the Middle Ages live again in their work — the exhilaration of Palm Sunday, the garlands of flowers, the bouquets fastened on the doors, the strewing of fresh herbs in the chapels, the magical flowers of the feast of Saint John — all the fleeting charm of those old-time springs and summers. The Middle Ages, so often said to have little love for

nature, in point of fact gazed at every blade of grass with reverence."

It is not merely love of nature but scientific interest and accuracy that we see revealed in the sculptures of the cathedrals and in the note-books of the thirteenth-century architect, Villard de Honnecourt, with its sketches of insect as well as animal life, of a lobster, two parroquets on a perch, the spirals of a snail's shell, a fly, a dragonfly, and a grasshopper, as well as a bear and a lion from life, and more familiar animals such as the cat and the swan. The sculptors of gargoyles and chimeras were not content to reproduce existing animals but showed their command of animal anatomy by creating strange compound and hybrid monsters — one might almost say, evolving new species — which nevertheless have all the verisimilitude of copies from living forms. It was these breeders in stone, these Burbanks of the pencil, these Darwins with the chisel, who knew nature and had studied botany and zoology in a way superior to the scholar who simply pored over the works of Aristotle and Pliny. No wonder that Albert's students were curious about particular things.

Finally, can we accept the altered concept of a Prenaissance as the vestibule to modern times and seed-bed of the modern spirit? Chronologically, perhaps. But, aside from the circumstance that modern times and spirit seem at present to be swiftly shifting, are not our political, economic, charitable, educational and ecclesiastical institutions quite as much an outgrowth from medieval life? Without attempting here to argue this larger question, I would merely recall that medieval men coined the word, modern, and regularly spoke of themselves or the last generations of themselves as such. "Maurus, Matthew, Solomon, Peter, Urso are modern physicians through whom reigns the medicine of Salerno." About 1050 Berengar of Tours was accused of "introducing ancient heresies in modern times"; about 1108 Hugh de Fleury wrote his Historia moderna. "On all sides they clamor," wrote John of Salisbury in the twelfth century, "what do we care for the sayings or deeds of the ancients? . . . The golden sayings of the ancients pleased their times; now only new ones please our times." When in the next century Robertus Anglicus composed his treatise on the quadrant, it was called *Tractatus quadrantis secundum modernos.* But then improvements were made in the quadrant and Robert's work became *Tractatus quadrantis veteris.* Even scholastic philosophy had its *via moderna* as well as *via antiqua.*

The concept of the Italian Renaissance or Prenaissance has in my opinion done a great deal of harm in the past and may continue to do harm in the future. It is too suggestive of a sensational, miraculous, extraordinary, magical, human and intellectual development, like unto the phoenix rising from its ashes after five hundred years. It is contrary to the fact that human nature tends to remain much the same in all times. It has led to a chorus of rhapsodists as to freedom, breadth, soaring ideas, horizons, perspectives, out of fetters and swaddling clothes, and so on. It long discouraged the study of centuries of human development that preceded it, and blinded the French *philosophes* and revolutionists to the value of medieval political and economic institutions. It has kept men in general from recognizing that our life and thought is based more nearly and actually on the middle ages than on distant Greece and Rome, from whom our heritage is more indirect, bookish and sentimental, less institutional, social, religious, even less economic and experimental.

But what is the use of questioning the Renaissance? No one has ever proved its existence; no one has really tried to. So often as one phase of it or conception of it is disproved, or is shown to be equally characteristic of the preceding period, its defenders take up a new position and are just as happy, just as enthusiastic, just as complacent as ever.

You may break, you may shatter the vase, if you will,
But the scent of the roses will hang round it still.

Still lingers the sweet perfume of the Renaissance; still hovers about us the blithe spirit of the Prenaissance.

THE RENAISSANCE AND ENGLISH HUMANISM: MODERN THEORIES OF THE RENAISSANCE

DOUGLAS BUSH

Douglas Bush is Professor of English Literature at Harvard University. The selection which follows is part of his first lecture given in 1939 under the provisions of the Alexander Lectureship in English of the University of Toronto. Ferguson considers his first lecture "an excellent general account, certainly the best in our language, of the history of the Renaissance concept."

A MORE recent religious interpretation of the Renaissance is that of Giuseppe Toffanin. For him individualism, in Burckhardt's sense of the word, is a late medieval phenomenon and a short-lived one. Toffanin sees classical humanism rising, not as a contributory cause of irreligious individualism, but as an anti-individualistic wall of learned orthodoxy. The spirit of the age of transition from medievalism to modernity is a faith in the progressive and final religious and cultural unity of the world under the auspices of classical humanism. Humanism has a bond of union with scholasticism, for both originated in an anti-democratic and anti-heretical impulse. Like scholasticism, humanism arrested for a time the eruption of the various rationalistic and naturalistic forces which we call modern. In concentrating on the Italian humanistic tradition, which many writers of late have tended to neglect or disparage, Toffanin may perhaps be charged, like other theorists, with a too narrow exclusiveness, yet to me at least the tradition of Christian humanism seems a broad and central road. Toffanin's view of a strong Italian orthodoxy is, I think, fundamentally sound, and one large result is the emergence of the true harmony,

rather than the conventional differences, between Italian and northern humanism. But this subject must be postponed for the present.

We may turn now to those theories which reject the notion of Italy as the matrix of the Renaissance. The only other country which can be set up as a rival is France — that is, pending an official proclamation from Germany of purely Teutonic origins. The significance of medieval French culture was already a commonplace in the time of Pater's volume, and some modern scholars have urged that the Renaissance was not Italian and of the fifteenth century, but French and of the twelfth. All the manifestations of ripe culture found in Italy, from conversation to cathedrals, are found in France at an earlier date — civilized towns and polished courts; cultivated society in which women play an important role; an abundant and sophisticated literature; achievements in the fine and useful arts; and so on. In many things, such as the romances of chivalry and the lyrical poetry of love, France is the teacher of Italy. Even the classical primacy of the Italians may be questioned. Old French literature shows wide and intelligent knowledge and adaptation of the Latin classics. The classical

From Douglas Bush, *The Renaissance and English Humanism* (Toronto, 1939), pp. 24–38. By permission of the University of Toronto Press.

revival under Charlemagne, which caused Bishop Modoin to exclaim that golden Rome was reborn for the world, was carried on in such centres as Chartres and flowered in the great renaissance of the twelfth century. This early renaissance was of major importance on the classical side and it was still more important in the development of philosophy, science, and mathematics. And all this fertile activity is going on in France before Italy is well awake. As even a summary partly indicates, this thesis can be carried to extreme lengths, as it has been by Johan Nordström, and we find a French scholar declaring, for instance, that until the sixteenth century English literature was hardly more than an offshoot of French! But even chauvinistic claims may have an ultimately salutary effect. We cannot ignore the international character of medieval culture and isolate the French or the Italian Renaissance as a purely self-contained phenomenon.

The various strands of our large problem are too closely interwoven to be kept separate and the question of Italian origins has already partly anticipated the question of chronology. We must have some rough chronological limits in mind when we use the word "Renaissance." Even if we use it to indicate an individual outlook and attitude we imply that there was some period when that outlook and attitude were characteristic and dominant, or as characteristic and dominant as a particular Weltanschauung ever is in any age. Burckhardt saw the Renaissance as beginning in Italy in the fourteenth century and reaching its climax around 1500. It was a simple matter for him, since Renaissance day banished medieval night, and the few gleams of individualism that he discerned in the Middle Ages, such as the Goliardic songs, were obviously the first rays of dawn. Michelet had already taken a wider view. He had in fact observed so many medieval expressions of individualism that he was compelled to ask why the Renaissance arrived three hundred years later than it should have. The answer seemed to be that the medieval

mind, entrenched behind its walls of religious conservatism and superstition, stubbornly resisted the forces making for a return to nature. Of later nineteenth-century historians, some saw the Middle Ages as a broad plain, without much on it but churches and monasteries, sloping up slightly from the early barbarian period and then rising suddenly to a mountain range. For others the plain was studded with hills, but they were the foothills of the Renaissance. When we stop to think of it, the term "Middle Ages," though both the phrase and the idea have a long pedigree, is unhistorical. It implies that a period of a thousand years, a fairly large segment in the recorded life of man, was not itself, an integral and consecutive part of the great panorama, but a sort of interlude between the two periods which really mattered. André Maurois somewhere caricatures the unhistorical attitude by having a knight address his followers in this fashion: "In truth, then, we men of the Middle Ages must not forget that tomorrow we set off for the Hundred Years' War."

One reason for the general readiness to play fast and loose with the Middle Ages has been the general ignorance which has prevailed until a relatively recent time. William Morris was a medieval enthusiast, with great knowledge in some directions, yet his conception of the medieval world was quite unrealistic. Of late years we have had the religious, social, and alcoholic romanticism of Chesterton and Belloc, the twin exponents of "the Mass and Maypole" school of history. And many secularly minded people still believe that the Middle Ages were romantic, though a medieval knight, sitting down at a modern breakfast-table beside a toaster and a percolator, would think he had been transported out of his own prosaic world into the land of Prester John. But the more serious fault of serious historians has been the drawing of picturesque contrasts between the religiosity of the Middle Ages and the paganism of the Renaissance. Symonds, for example, can indulge in a paragraph like this, in which you will observe, incidentally, the usual echoes of Michelet:

During the Middle Ages man had lived enveloped in a cowl. He had not even seen the beauty of the world, or had seen it only to cross himself, and turn aside and tell his beads and pray; . . . humanity had passed, a careful pilgrim, intent on the terrors of sin, death, and judgment, along the highways of the world, and had scarcely known that they were sightworthy or that life is a blessing. Beauty is a snare, pleasure a sin, the world a fleeting show, man fallen and lost, death the only certainty, judgment inevitable, hell everlasting, heaven hard to win; ignorance is acceptable to God as a proof of faith and submission; abstinence and mortification are the only safe rules of life: these were the fixed ideas of the ascetic mediaeval Church. The Renaissance shattered and destroyed them, rending the thick veil which they had drawn between the mind of man and the outer world, and flashing the light of reality upon the darkened places of his own nature. For the mystic teaching of the Church was substituted culture in the classical humanities; a new ideal was established, whereby man strove to make himself the monarch of the globe on which it is his privilege as well as his destiny to live. The Renaissance was the liberation of the reason from a dungeon, the double discovery of the outer and the inner world.

At least we should acknowledge that Jean de Meung and Chaucer wore their cowls with a difference, even if they did not enjoy life like Savonarola and Calvin.

To return to the specific problem of chronology, modern critics may be roughly divided into two camps. One view extends the Renaissance backward to include the Middle Ages, the other extends the Middle Ages forward to include the Renaissance. It may serve as a useful warning of my own set of prejudices if I say that I incline to the latter. These two groups often appear in unnecessarily rigid opposition, when logic as well as history would recommend a compromise, but they have one basic attitude in common: they do insist on an historical continuity which makes the Middle Ages and the Renaissance much more alike than they used to be thought. The great

watershed of the Renaissance has been, if not levelled down, at any rate made a less conspicuous eminence than it was. If we take the metaphysical view of man and the universe to be the most fundamental criterion, some scholars would say that the later Middle Ages and the seventeenth century witnessed more essential and far-reaching changes than the intervening period. The wholesale introduction of Aristotle in the twelfth century enabled St. Thomas Aquinas to build his great structure of rational theology; it also started the stream of scientific rationalism which was to undermine that structure; and these two movements, especially the latter, may be said to have given the modern mind its direction. At the same time, to be indecisively and exasperatingly judicial, undue insistence on continuity and undue depreciation of the Renaissance may result in missing the woods for the trees, in blurring really significant alterations in the contours of the spiritual landscape. There has been a danger in modern scholarship, a danger which is perhaps being illustrated in these discourses, but our concern at the moment is with the older attitude which brought on the reaction just described.

Depreciation of the Middle Ages has had a number of more or less traditional reasons behind it. One has been noticed, the lack of real knowledge and understanding of medieval culture. Another reason is that historians have been over-ready to take at its face value the scorn which many Renaissance humanists and neoclassicists felt for things medieval, such as degenerate scholasticism and Gothic art. A future historian would be injudicious if he allowed his estimate of the Victorian age to be guided by twentieth-century rebels against effete Victorianism. Thirdly, there has come down from the sixteenth and seventeenth centuries a considerable Protestant prejudice against the Catholic Middle Ages. Finally, and perhaps chiefly, the Michelet-Burckhardt conception of the Renaissance, which has been so congenial to the modern mind, while it was, to be sure, based on historical research, was also largely predetermined by the philosophic outlook of its authors. It was, in short, a conception engendered by modern secular liberalism, by the nineteenth-century faith in rationalistic enlightenment and progress. From that point of view the Middle Ages appeared as not much more than a long cultural lag, a period in which man was enslaved by a system based on religious superstition and unnatural restraint. Hence anything in the way of revolt was a step toward the Renaissance and, ultimately, toward the triumphant freedom of the nineteenth century.

As I have remarked already, Burckhardt's conception of the Renaissance is still the popular one, and there are still scholars who celebrate the secularizing of the human mind, its emancipation from the shackles of superstition. But nowadays such verdicts command less immediate assent than they once did. As we look around our world and consider where the emancipated mind has landed us, we may think that liberal historians might be a little less complacent about progress. And, in spite of our long subservience to secular liberalism, the climate of opinion in some quarters has changed a good deal. Voices can be heard declaring that the Renaissance, so far as it involved a secular revolt, was more of a calamity than a triumph. Our concern, however, is with less nostalgic and more historical ideas. On the one hand we might defend the Middle Ages by saying that they were full of rebels against religious, ethical, social, and political authority. But such a defence, though obvious and true, is not the one I would choose to offer. The Middle Ages can rest sufficient claims to greatness on their leaders of orthodoxy, however important the rebels may have been. On the other hand, until quite recent times historians, partly through prejudice and partly through ignorance, have much exaggerated the suddenness and completeness of the Renaissance emancipation from medievalism. Since these lectures will be largely occupied with some Good Things which the Renaissance inherited from the Middle

Ages, we can afford to admit that many Bad Things also survived. The so-called enlightenment did not banish astrology and witchcraft; indeed such sciences flourished with fresh vigour. And countless other irrational and uncritical beliefs and habits of mind persisted not merely among the multitude but among the educated, including such heralds of modernity as Bodin and Bacon and Descartes.

It is self-evident that the Renaissance, even in its narrower meaning of a classical revival, was a heterogeneous movement which contained many mutually antagonistic impulses. Without forgetting the various pitfalls of generalization we have encountered, and without denying the importance, the necessity, of the rebellious side of the Renaissance, I wish in these discussions to emphasize the more neglected and, I think, more truly representative elements of orthodox conservatism. That means, of course, emphasis on the continued strength of medieval attitudes and ways of thought, in union with a richer and fuller appreciation of the classics than medieval men ordinarily possessed. To put the matter briefly and somewhat too bluntly, in the Renaissance the ancient pagan tradition (which does not mean neopaganism), with all its added power, did not overthrow the medieval Christian tradition; it was rather, in the same way if not quite to the same degree as in the Middle Ages, absorbed by the Christian tradition. And that, after all, is only what we would, or should, expect.

If we are more accustomed to think of the Renaissance in terms of emancipation and rebellion and are more familiar with the rebels than with the conservatives, it is partly because all the world loves a rebel and partly, as I have said, because the historians have stressed what appealed to them. We look at the voluptuous Venuses of the Italian painters and exclaim, "How typical of the Renaissance lust of the eye and pride of life!" But why are they more typical than the multitudinous Madonnas of the same period? For one person who has heard of Vittorino da Feltre, the Christian humanist whose teaching flowered in the culture of Urbino, a score have heard of that really insignificant scoundrel, Pietro Aretino. It is a cliché of English literary history that Marlowe is the very incarnation of the pagan Renaissance. But is Marlowe's half-boyish revolt against traditional faith and morality more, or less, typical and important than Hooker's majestic exposition of the workings of divine reason in divine and human law?

Before we leave general definitions of the Renaissance for classical humanism, I should like to dwell a bit longer on the theory of individualism. There is not much time for it, but one may ask a few questions. In the first place, was the medieval church so crushing a weight upon the individual? One might reply that Chaucer's pilgrims do not seem to feel crushed. On a more philosophic if not necessarily a more convincing level one might appeal to the thoroughgoing moral individualism of Aquinas. It is dubious history as well as dubious praise to claim for the Renaissance the distinction of having established immoral individualism. If that were true, the medieval church would have had an easier task than it had.

But, it may be said, was not Protestantism itself the expression of Renaissance individualism *par excellence?* While on the one hand Protestantism made every man his own priest, on the other it substituted the absolute authority of the church. And if in practice the medieval church was often repressive, it was less so than Protestantism, as soon as the latter achieved organization and power. Besides, we must remember that the Reformation was only the climax of a widespread medieval movement; Luther's chief guides, apart from the Bible, were Augustine and medieval pietists.

In the field of political thought there is the bogeyman of Europe, the exponent of unscrupulous Italian individualism. Machiavelli was a conscientious official and ardent patriot who was daring enough to find lessons for his troubled time and country in the pages of Livy. His ideal was not the

despotism of the ruthless strong man, it was the ancient Roman republic; but he believed that despotism might be a necessary prelude to a republic, since only the strong man could create order out of chaos. Machiavelli's view of the state, as his avowed modern disciple has realized, has much in common with Fascism. Further, his supposedly revolutionary doctrine of expediency was in the main a formulation of the principles on which medieval statecraft had operated. As Professor J. W. Allen remarks, in connection with Machiavelli, the further you go into the political thought of the sixteenth century, the more medieval you will find it.

In the field of personal ethics there is that philosophic individualist, Montaigne, who devotes his life to the study of himself as he is, without excuses and without unduly exacting aspirations, and who seems to be, in his quiet ironic way, a solvent of all traditional external restraints. Yet, although Montaigne draws his rationalism from the classics and from himself, he respects religion as a plane of experience above his own. And he is a good if not over-active Catholic, partly by instinct and inheritance, but much more because he believes in the necessity and efficacy of the church as a bulwark of solidarity. Moreover, if Montaigne secularizes personal ethics, he is no modern advocate of "self-expression." He had a large share in creating the ideal of the *honnete homme,* and the very definition of the civilized man is that he obeys standards of good taste, a norm of rational behaviour free from individual eccentricities. Thus, however much Montaigne might be invoked by *libertins,* he is to be found on the side of order, authority, reason. His essays may be called, in the words of Lanson (who makes due qualifications), the great reservoir from which is to flow the classic spirit. . . .

Altogether, our theory of the Renaissance must be, like the Copernican hypothesis, the simplest theory which explains the phenomena. That of rebellious individualism is much too simple and exclusive.

THE RENAISSANCE OF THE TWELFTH CENTURY

CHARLES HOMER HASKINS

Charles Homer Haskins (1870–1937) is remembered by many as a profound scholar, a great teacher, and a respected author and editor. Educated at Johns Hopkins University, he was a member of its faculty until 1902 when he became Professor of History at Harvard University. At this latter university he served for many years as Dean of The Graduate School of Arts and Sciences. His scholarship and publications in the field of medieval history were recognized when he was elected to the presidency of the Mediaeval Academy of America in 1926. He also served as editor of The American Historical Series.

PREFACE

The title of this book will appear to many to contain a flagrant contradiction. A renaissance in the twelfth century! Do not the Middle Ages, that epoch of ignorance, stagnation, and gloom, stand in the sharpest contrast to the light and progress and freedom of the Italian Renaissance which followed? How could there be a renaissance in the Middle Ages, when men had no eye for the joy and beauty and knowledge of this passing world, their gaze ever fixed on the terrors of the world to come? Is not this whole period summed up in Symonds' picture of St. Bernard, blind to the beauties of Lake Leman as he bends "a thought-burdened forehead over the neck of his mule," typical of an age when "humanity had passed, a careful pilgrim, intent on the terrors of sin, death, and judgment, along the highways of the world, and had scarcely known that they were sightworthy, or that life is a blessing"?

The answer is that the continuity of history rejects such sharp and violent contrasts between successive periods, and that modern research shows us the Middle Ages less dark and less static, the Renaissance less bright and less sudden, than was once supposed. The Middle Ages exhibit life and color and change, much eager search after knowledge and beauty, much creative accomplishment in art, in literature, in institutions. The Italian Renaissance was preceded by similar, if less wide-reaching movements; indeed it came out of the Middle Ages so gradually that historians are not agreed when it began, and some would go so far as to abolish the name, and perhaps even the fact, of a renaissance in the Quattrocento.

To the most important of these earlier revivals the present volume is devoted, the Renaissance of the Twelfth Century which is often called the mediaeval Renaissance. This century, the very century of St. Bernard and his mule, was in many respects an age of fresh and vigorous life. The epoch of the Crusades, of the rise of towns, and of the earliest bureaucratic states of the West, it saw the culmination of Romanesque art and the beginnings of Gothic;

Reprinted by permission of the publishers from C. H. Haskins, *The Renaissance of the Twelfth Century,* Cambridge, Mass.: Harvard University Press, 1927 and 1955, pp. vii–ix, 3–12, by Clare Allen Haskins and The President and Fellows of Harvard College.

the emergence of the vernacular literatures; the revival of the Latin classics and of Latin poetry and Roman law; the recovery of Greek science, with its Arabic additions, and of much of Greek philosophy; and the origin of the first European universities. The twelfth century left its signature on higher education, on the scholastic philosophy, on European systems of law, on architecture and sculpture, on the liturgical drama, on Latin and vernacular poetry. The theme is too broad for a single volume, or a single author. Accordingly, since the art and the vernacular literature of the epoch are better known, we shall confine ourselves to the Latin side of this renaissance, the revival of learning in the broadest sense — the Latin classics and their influence, the new jurisprudence and the more varied historiography, the new knowledge of the Greeks and Arabs and its effects upon Western science and philosophy, and the new institutions of learning, all seen against the background of the century's centres and materials of culture. The absence of any other work on this general theme must be the author's excuse for attempting a sketch where much must necessarily rest upon second hand information. . . .

THE HISTORICAL BACKGROUND

The European Middle Ages form a complex and varied as well as a very considerable period of human history. Within their thousand years of time they include a large variety of peoples, institutions, and types of culture, illustrating many processes of historical development and containing the origins of many phases of modern civilization. Contrasts of East and West, of the North and the Mediterranean, of old and new, sacred and profane, ideal and actual, give life and color and movement to this period, while its close relations alike to antiquity and to the modern world assure it a place in the continuous history of human development. Both continuity and change are characteristic of the Middle Ages, as indeed of all great epochs of history.

This conception runs counter to ideas widely prevalent not only among the unlearned but among many who ought to know better. To these the Middle Ages are synonymous with all that is uniform, static, and unprogressive; "mediaeval" is applied to anything outgrown, until, as Bernard Shaw reminds us, even the fashion plates of the preceding generation are pronounced "mediaeval." The barbarism of Goths and Vandals is thus spread out over the following centuries, even to that "Gothic" architecture which is one of the crowning achievements of the constructive genius of the race; the ignorance and superstition of this age are contrasted with the enlightenment of the Renaissance, in strange disregard of the alchemy and demonology which flourished throughout this succeeding period; and the phrase "Dark Ages" is extended to cover all that came between, let us say, 476 and 1453. Even those who realize that the Middle Ages are not "dark" often think of them as uniform, at least during the central period from ca. 800 to ca. 1300, distinguished by the great mediaeval institutions of feudalism, ecclesiasticism, and scholasticism, and preceded and followed by epochs of more rapid transformation. Such a view ignores the unequal development of different parts of Europe, the great economic changes within this epoch, the influx of the new learning of the East, the shifting currents in the stream of mediaeval life and thought. On the intellectual side, in particular, it neglects the mediaeval revival of the Latin classics and of jurisprudence, the extension of knowledge by the absorption of ancient learning and by observation, and the creative work of these centuries in poetry and in art. In many ways the differences between the Europe of 800 and that of 1300 are greater than the resemblances. Similar contrasts, though on a smaller scale, can be made between the culture of the eighth and the ninth centuries, between conditions ca. 1100 and those ca. 1200, between the preceding age and the new intellectual currents of the thirteenth and fourteenth centuries.

For convenience' sake it has become common to designate certain of these movements as the Carolingian Renaissance, the Ottonian Renaissance, the Renaissance of the Twelfth Century, after the fashion of the phrase once reserved exclusively for the Italian Renaissance of the fifteenth century. Some, it is true, would give up the word renaissance altogether, as conveying false impressions of a sudden change and an original and distinct culture in the fifteenth century, and, in general, as implying that there ever can be a real revival of something past; Mr. Henry Osborn Taylor prides himself on writing two volumes on *Thought and Expression in the Sixteenth Century* without once using this forbidden term. Nevertheless, it may be doubted whether such a term is more open to misinterpretation than others, like the Quattrocento or the sixteenth century, and it is so convenient and so well established that, like Austria, if it had not existed we should have to invent it. There was an Italian Renaissance, whatever we choose to call it, and nothing is gained by the process which ascribes the Homeric poems to another poet of the same name. But — thus much we must grant — the great Renaissance was not so unique or so decisive as has been supposed. The contrast of culture was not nearly so sharp as it seemed to the humanists and their modern followers, while within the Middle Ages there were intellectual revivals whose influence was not lost to succeeding times, and which partook of the same character as the better known movement of the fifteenth century. To one of these this volume is devoted, the Renaissance of the Twelfth Century, which is also known as the Mediaeval Renaissance.

The renaissance of the twelfth century might conceivably be taken so broadly as to cover all the changes through which Europe passed in the hundred years or more from the late eleventh century to the taking of Constantinople by the Latins in 1204 and the contemporary events which usher in the thirteenth century, just as we speak of the Age of the Renaissance in later Italy; but such a view becomes too wide and vague for any purpose save the general history of the period. More profitably we may limit the phrase to the history of culture in this age — the complete development of Romanesque art and the rise of Gothic; the full bloom of vernacular poetry, both lyric and epic; and the new learning and new literature in Latin. The century begins with the flourishing age of the cathedral schools and closes with the earliest universities already well established at Salerno, Bologna, Paris, Montpellier, and Oxford. It starts with only the bare outlines of the seven liberal arts and ends in possession of the Roman and canon law, the new Aristotle, the new Euclid and Ptolemy, and the Greek and Arabic physicians, thus making possible a new philosophy and a new science. It sees a revival of the Latin classics, of Latin prose, and of Latin verse, both in the ancient style of Hildebert and the new rhymes of the Goliardi, and the formation of the liturgical drama. New activity in historical writing reflects the variety and amplitude of a richer age — biography, memoir, court annals, the vernacular history, and the city chronicle. A library of *ca.* 1100 would have little beyond the Bible and the Latin Fathers, with their Carolingian commentators, the service books of the church and various lives of saints, the textbooks of Boethius and some others, bits of local history, and perhaps certain of the Latin classics, too often covered with dust. About 1200, or a few years later, we should expect to find, not only more and better copies of these older works, but also the Corpus Juris Civilis and the classics partially rescued from neglect; the canonical collections of Gratian and the recent Popes, the theology of Anselm and Peter Lombard and the other early scholastics; the writings of St. Bernard and other monastic leaders (a good quarter of the two hundred and seventeen volumes of the Latin *Patrologia* belong to this period); a mass of new history, poetry, and correspondence; the philosophy, mathematics, and astronomy unknown to the earlier mediaeval tradition and recovered from the Greeks and Arabs in the course of the twelfth century. We should now have the great feudal epics of France and the best of the Provençal lyrics, as well as the earliest works in Middle High German. Romanesque art would have reached and passed its prime, and the new Gothic style would be firmly established at Paris, Chartres, and lesser centres in the Île de France.

A survey of the whole Western culture of the twelfth century would take us far afield, and in many directions the preliminary studies are still lacking. The limits of the present volume, and of its author's knowledge, compel us to leave aside the architecture and sculpture of the age, as well as its vernacular literature, and concentrate our attention upon the Latin writings of the period and what of its life and thought they reveal. Art and literature are never wholly distinct, and Latin and vernacular cannot, of course, be sharply separated, for they run on lines which are often parallel and often cross or converge, and we are learning that it is quite impossible to maintain the watertight compartments which were once thought to separate the writings of the learned and unlearned. The interpenetration of these two literatures must constantly be kept in mind. Nevertheless, the two are capable of separate discussion, and, since far more attention has been given to the vernacular, justification is not hard to find for a treatment of the more specifically Latin Renaissance.

Chronological limits are not easy to set. Centuries are at best but arbitrary conveniences which must not be permitted to clog or distort our historical thinking: history cannot remain history if sawed off into even lengths of hundreds of years. The most that can be said is that the later eleventh century shows many signs of new life, political, economic, religious, intellectual, for which, like the revival of Roman law and the new interest in the classics, specific dates can rarely be assigned, and that, if we were to choose the First Crusade in 1096 as a convenient turning-point, it must be with a full realization that this particular event has in itself no decisive importance in intellectual history, and that the real change began some fifty years earlier. At the latter end the period is even less sharply defined. Once requickened, intellectual life did not slacken or abruptly change its character. The fourteenth century grows out of the thirteenth as the thirteenth grows out of the twelfth, so that there is no real break between the mediaeval renaissance and the Quattrocento. Dante, an undergraduate once declared, "stands with one foot in the Middle Ages while with the other he salutes the rising star of the Renaissance"! If the signature of the thirteenth century is easy to recognize in the literature, art, and thought of ca. 1250, as contrasted with the more fluid and formative epoch which precedes, no sharp line of demarcation separates the two. We can only say that, about the turn of the century, the fall of the Greek empire, the reception of the new Aristotle, the triumph of logic over letters, and the decline of the creative period in Latin and French poetry, mark a transition which we cannot overlook, while two generations later the new science and philosophy have been reduced to order by Albertus Magnus and Thomas Aquinas. By 1200 the mediaeval renaissance is well advanced, by 1250 its work is largely done. In a phrase like "the renaissance of the twelfth century," the word "century" must be used very loosely so as to cover not only the twelfth century proper but the years which immediately precede and follow, yet with sufficient emphasis on the central period to indicate the outstanding characteristics of its civilization. For the movement as a whole we must really go back fifty years or more and forward almost as far.

Furthermore, the various phases of the movement do not exactly synchronize, just as in the later Renaissance there is not complete parallelism between the revival of classical learning, the outburst of Italian art, and the discoveries of Columbus and Copernicus. Certainly the revival of the Latin classics begins in the eleventh century, if indeed it may not be regarded as a continuous advance since Carolingian times, while the force of the new humanism is largely spent before the twelfth century is over. The new science, on the other hand, does not start before the second quarter of the twelfth century, and once begun it goes on into the thirteenth century in unbroken continuity, at least until the absorption of Greek and Arabic learning is completed. The philosophical revival which starts in the twelfth century has its culmination in the thirteenth. Here, as throughout all history, no single date possesses equal importance in all lines of development.

Unlike the Carolingian Renaissance, the revival of the twelfth century was not the product of a court or a dynasty; and unlike the Italian Renaissance, it owed its beginning to no single country. If Italy had its part, as regards Roman and canon law and the translations from the Greek, it was not the decisive part, save in the field of law. France, on the whole, was more important, with its monks and philosophers, its cathedral schools culminating in the new University of Paris, its Goliardi and vernacular poets, its central place in the new Gothic art. England and Germany are noteworthy, though in the spread of culture from France and Italy rather than in its origination; in-deed, the period in Germany is in some respects one of decline as we approach the thirteenth century, while England moves forward in the closest relation with France, as regards both Latin and vernacular culture. Spain's part was to serve as the chief link with the learning of the Mohammedan world; the very names of the translators who worked there illustrate the European character of the new search for learning: John of Seville, Hugh of Santalla, Plato of Tivoli, Gerard of Cremona, Hermann of Carinthia, Rudolf of Bruges, Robert of Chester, and the rest. Christian Spain was merely a transmitter to the North.

Such names, for the most part only names to us, suggest that the twelfth century lacks the wealth and variety of striking personalities in which the Italian Renaissance abounds. It has no such mass of memoirs and correspondence, its outstanding individuals are relatively few. Nor can it claim the artistic interest of portraiture. Its art is rich and distinctive both in sculpture and architecture, but it is an art of types, not of individuals. It has left us no portraits of scholars or men of letters, very few even of rulers or prelates. It has not even given us likenesses of its horses, such as adorn the palace of the Gonzaga dukes at Mantua.

THE WANING OF THE MIDDLE AGES

JOHAN HUIZINGA

Johan Huizinga (1872–1945), the Dutch historian, served as professor of history at the universities of Gröningen and Leyden. A capacity for projecting himself imaginatively into historical ages and personalities, makes his writings reveal deep impressions of the spirit and inner life of the subject he was describing. His contributions to cultural history were great and his artistic style and impressionistic manner remind one of Burckhardt.

ACCORDING to the celebrated Swiss historian, the quest of personal glory was the characteristic attribute of the men of the Renaissance. The Middle Ages proper, according to him, knew honour and glory only in collective forms, as the honour due to groups and orders of society, the honour of rank, of class, or of profession. It was in Italy, he thinks, under the influence of antique models, that the craving for individual glory originated. Here, as elsewhere, Burckhardt has exaggerated the distance separating Italy from the Western countries and the Renaissance from the Middle Ages.

The thirst for honour and glory proper to the men of the Renaissance is essentially the same as the chivalrous ambition of earlier times, and of French origin. Only it has shaken off the feudal garb. The passionate desire to find himself praised by contemporaries or by posterity was the source of virtue with the courtly knight of the twelfth century and the rude captain of the fourteenth, no less than with the beaux-esprits of the quattrocento. When Beaumanoir and Bamborough fix the conditions of the famous combat of the Thirty, the English captain, according to Froissart, expresses himself in these terms: "And let us

right there try ourselves and do so much that people will speak of it in future times in halls, in palaces, in public places and elsewhere throughout the world." The saying may not be authentic, but it teaches what Froissart thought.

The quest of glory and of honour goes hand in hand with a hero-worship which also might seem to announce the Renaissance. The somewhat factitious revival of the splendour of chivalry that we find everywhere in European courts after 1300 is already connected with the Renaissance by a real link. It is a naïve prelude to it. In reviving chivalry the poets and princes imagined that they were returning to antiquity. In the minds of the fourteenth century, a vision of antiquity had hardly yet disengaged itself from the fairy-land sphere of the Round Table. Classical heroes were still tinged with the general colour of romance. On the one hand, the figure of Alexander had long ago entered the sphere of chivalry; on the other chivalry was supposed to be of Roman origin. "And he maintained the discipline of chivalry well, as did the Romans formerly," thus a Burgundian chronicler praised Henry V of England. The blazons of Caesar, of Hercules, and of Troilus, are placed in a fantasy of King

From J. Huizinga, *The Waning of the Middle Ages* (London, 1948), pp. 58–60, 297–308. By permission of Edward Arnold and Co. The English translations of the French passages have been taken from the footnotes of the book.

René, side by side with those of Arthur and of Lancelot. Certain coincidences of terminology played a part in tracing back the origin of chivalry to Roman antiquity. How could people have known that the word *miles* with Roman authors did not mean a *miles* in the sense of medieval Latin, that is to say, a knight, or that a Roman *eques* differed from a feudal knight? Consequently, Romulus, because he raised a band of a thousand mounted warriors, was taken to be the founder of chivalry.

The life of a knight is an imitation; that of princes is so too, sometimes. No one was so consciously inspired by models of the past, or manifested such desire to rival them, as Charles the Bold. In his youth he made his attendants read out to him the exploits of Gauvain and of Lancelot. Later he preferred the ancients. Before retiring to rest, he listens for an hour or two to the "lofty histories of Rome." He especially admires Caesar, Hannibal and Alexander, "whom he wished to follow and imitate." All his contemporaries attach great importance to this eagerness to imitate the heroes of antiquity, and agree in regarding it as the mainspring of his conduct. "He desired great glory" — says Commines — "which more than anything else led him to undertake his wars; and longed to resemble those ancient princes who have been so much talked of after their death." The anecdote is well known of the jester who, after the defeat of Granson, called out to him: "My lord, we are well Hannibaled this time!" . . .

Thus the aspiration to the splendour of antique life, which is the characteristic of the Renaissance, has its roots in the chivalrous ideal. Between the ponderous spirit of the Burgundian and the classical instinct of an Italian of the same period there is only a difference of nuance. The forms which Charles the Bold affected are still flamboyant Gothic, and he still read his classics in translations.

THE ADVENT OF THE NEW FORM

The transition from the spirit of the declining Middle Ages to humanism was far less simple than we are inclined to imagine it. Accustomed to oppose humanism to the Middle Ages, we would gladly believe that it was necessary to give up the one in order to embrace the other. We find it difficult to fancy the mind cultivating the ancient forms of medieval thought and expression while aspiring at the same time to antique wisdom and beauty. Yet this is just what we have to picture to ourselves. Classicism did not come as a sudden revelation, it grew up among the luxuriant vegetation of medieval thought. Humanism was a form before it was an inspiration. On the other hand, the characteristic modes of thought of the Middle Ages did not die out till long after the Renaissance.

In Italy the problem of humanism presents itself in a most simple form, because there men's minds had ever been predisposed to the reception of antique culture. The Italian spirit had never lost touch with classic harmony and simplicity. It could expand freely and naturally in the restored forms of classic expression. The quattrocento with its serenity makes the impression of a renewed culture, which has shaken off the fetters of medieval thought, until Savonarola reminds us that below the surface the Middle Ages still subsist.

The history of French civilization of the fifteenth century, on the contrary, does not permit us to forget the Middle Ages. France had been the mother-land of all that was strongest and most beautiful in the products of the medieval spirit. All medieval forms — feudalism, the ideas of chivalry and courtesy, scholasticism, Gothic architecture — were rooted here much more firmly than ever they had been in Italy. In the fifteenth century they were dominating still. Instead of the full rich style, the blitheness and the harmony characteristic of Italy and the Renaissance, here it is bizarre pomp, cumbrous forms of expression, a worn-out fancy and an atmosphere of melancholy gravity which prevail. It is not the Middle Ages, it is the new coming culture, which might easily be forgotten.

In literature classical forms could appear

without the spirit having changed. An interest in the refinement of Latin style was enough, it seems, to give birth to humanism. The proof of this is furnished by a group of French scholars about the year 1400. It was composed of ecclesiastics and magistrates, Jean de Monstreuil, canon of Lille and secretary to the king, Nicolas de Clemanges, the famous denouncer of abuses in the Church, Pierre et Gontier Col, the Milanese Ambrose de Miliis, also royal secretaries. The elegant and grave epistles they exchange are inferior in no respect — neither in the vagueness of thought, nor in the consequential air, not in the tortured sentences, nor even in learned trifling — to the epistolary genre of later humanists. Jean de Monstreuil spins long dissertations on the subject of Latin spelling. He defends Cicero and Virgil against the criticism of his friend Ambrose de Miliis, who had accused the former of contradictions and preferred Ovid to the latter. On another occasion he writes to Clemanges: "If you do not come to my aid, dear master and brother, I shall have lost my reputation and be as one sentenced to death. I have just noticed that in my last letter to my lord and father, the bishop of Cambray, I wrote *proximior* instead of the comparative *propior;* so rash and careless is the pen. Kindly correct this, otherwise our detractors will write libels about it." . . .

It suffices to recall that we met Jean de Monstreuil and the brothers Col among the zealots of the *Roman de la Rose* and among the members of the Court of Love of 1401, to be convinced that this primitive French humanism was but a secondary element of their culture, the fruit of scholarly erudition, analogous to the so-called renaissance of classic latinity of earlier ages, notably the ninth and the twelfth century. The circle of Jean de Monstreuil had no immediate successors, and this early French humanism seems to disappear with the men who cultivated it. Still, in its origins it was to some extent connected with the great international movement of literary renovation. Petrarch was, in the eyes of Jean de Monstreuil and his friends, the illustrious initia-

tor, and Coluccio Salutati, the Florentine chancellor who introduced classicism into official style, was not unknown to them either. Their zeal for classic refinement had evidently been roused not a little by Petrarch's taunt that there were no orators nor poets outside Italy. In France Petrarch's work had, so to say, been accepted in a medieval spirit and incorporated into medieval thought. He himself had personally known the leading spirits of the second half of the fourteenth century; the poet Philippe de Vitri, Nicholas Oresme, philosopher and politician, who had been a preceptor to the dauphin, probably also Philippe de Mézières. These men, in spite of the ideas which make Oresme one of the forerunners of modern science, were not humanists. As to Petrarch himself, we are always inclined to exaggerate the modern element in his mind and work, because we are accustomed to see him exclusively as the first of renovators. It is easy to imagine him emancipated from the ideas of his century. Nothing is further from the truth. He is most emphatically a man of his time. The themes of which he treated were those of the Middle Ages: *De contemptu mundi, De otio religiosorum, De vita solitaria.* It is only the form and the tone of his work which differ and are more highly finished. His glorification of antique virtue in his *De viris illustribus* and his *Rerum memorandarum libri* corresponds more or less with the chivalrous cult of the Nine Worthies. There is nothing surprising in his being found in touch with the founder of the Brethren of the Common Life, or cited as an authority on a dogmatic point by the fanatic Jean de Varennes. Denis the Carthusian borrowed laments from him about the loss of the Holy Sepulchre, a typically medieval subject. What contemporaries outside Italy saw in Petrarch was not at all the poet of the Sonnets or the *Trionfi,* but a moral philosopher, a Christian Cicero.

In a more limited field Boccaccio exercised an influence resembling that of Petrarch. His fame too was that of a moral philosopher, and by no means rested on the *Decamerone.* He was honoured as the "doctor of patience in adversity," as the author of *De casibus virorum illustrium* and of *De claris mulieribus*. Because of these queer writings treating of the inconstancy of human fate "messire Jehan Bococe" had made himself a sort of *impresario* of Fortune. As such he appears to Chastellain, who gave the name of *Le Temple de Bocace* to the bizarre treatise in which he endeavoured to console Queen Margaret, after her flight from England, by relating to her a series of the tragic destinies of his time. In recognizing in Boccaccio the strongly medieval spirit which was their own, these Burgundian spirits of a century later were not at all off the mark.

What distinguishes nascent Humanism in France from that of Italy, is a difference of erudition, skill and taste, rather than of tone or aspiration. To transplant antique form and sentiment into national literature the French had to overcome far more obstacles than the people born under the Tuscan sky or in the shadow of the Coliseum. France too, had her learned clerks, writing in Latin, who were capable at an early date of rising to the height of the epistolary style. But a blending of classicism and medievalism in the vernacular, such as was achieved by Boccaccio, was for a long time impossible in France. The old forms were too strong, and the general culture still lacked the proficiency in mythology and ancient history which was current in Italy. Machaut, although a clerk, pitifully disfigures the names of the seven sages. Chastellain confounds Peleus with Pelias, La Marche Proteus with Pirithous. The author of the *Pastoralet* speaks of the "good king Scipio of Africa." But at the same time his subject inspires him with a description of the god Silvanus and a prayer to Pan, in which the poetical imagination of the Renaissance seems on the point of breaking forth. The chroniclers were already trying their hand at military speeches in Livy's manner, and adorning their narrative of important events by mentioning portents, in close imitation of Livy. Their attempts at classicism did not always succeed. Jean

Germain's description of the Arras congress of 1435 is a veritable caricature of antique prose. The vision of Antiquity was still very bizarre. . . .

In so far as the French humanists of the fifteenth century wrote in Latin, the medieval subsoil of their culture is little in evidence. The more completely the classical style is imitated, the more the true spirit is concealed. The letters and the discourses of Robert Gaguin are not distinguishable from the works of other humanists. But Gaguin is, at the same time, a French poet of altogether medieval inspiration and of altogether national style. Whereas those who did not, and perhaps could not, write in Latin, spoiled their French by latinized forms, he, the accomplished latinist, when writing in French, disdained rhetorical effects. His *Débat du Laboureur, du Prestre et du Gendarme,* medieval in its subject, is also medieval in style. It is simple and vigorous, like Villon's poetry and Deschamps' best work. . . .

Classicism then was not the controlling factor in the advent of the new spirit in literature. Neither was paganism. The frequent use of pagan expressions or trophies has often been considered the chief characteristic of the Renaissance. This practice, however, is far older. As early as the twelfth century mythological terms were employed to express concepts of the Christian faith, and this was not considered at all irreverent or impious. Deschamps speaking of "Jupiter come from paradise," Villon calling the Holy Virgin "high goddess," the humanists referring to God in terms like "princeps superum" and to Mary as "genetrix tonantis," are by no means pagans. Pastorals required some admixture of innocent paganism, by which no reader was duped. The author of the *Pastoralet* who calls the Celestine church at Paris "the temple in the high woods, where people pray to the gods," declares, to dispel all ambiguity, "If, to lend my Muse some strangeness, I speak of the pagan gods, the shepherds and myself are Christians all the same." In the same way Molinet excuses himself for having introduced Mars and Minerva, by quoting "Reason and Understanding," who said to him: "You should do it, not to instil faith in gods and goddesses, but because Our Lord alone inspires people as it pleases Him and frequently by various inspirations.". . .

To find paganism, there was no need for the spirit of the waning Middle Ages to revert to classic literature. The pagan spirit displayed itself, as amply as possible, in the *Roman de la Rose*. Not in the guise of some mythological phrases; it was not there that the danger lay, but in the whole erotic conception and inspiration of this most popular work of all. From the early Middle Ages onward Venus and Cupid had found a refuge in this domain. But the great pagan who called them to vigorous life and enthroned them was Jean de Meun. By blending with Christian conceptions of eternal bliss the boldest praise of voluptuousness, he had taught numerous generations a very ambiguous attitude towards Faith. He had dared to distort Genesis for his impious purposes by making Nature complain of men because they neglect her commandment of procreation, in the words:

> So help me God who was crucified,
> I much repent that I made man.

It is astonishing that the Church, which so rigorously repressed the slightest deviations from dogma of a speculative character, suffered the teaching of this breviary of the aristocracy (for the *Roman de la Rose* was nothing less) to be disseminated with impunity.

But the essence of the great renewal lies even less in paganism than in pure Latinity. Classic expression and imagery, and even sentiments borrowed from heathen Antiquity, might be a potent stimulus or an indispensable support in the process of cultural renovation, they never were its moving power. The soul of Western Christendom itself was outgrowing medieval forms and modes of thought that had become shackles. The Middle Ages had always lived in the shadow of Antiquity, always handled its treasures, or what they had of them, interpreting it according to truly medieval principles: scholastic theology and chivalry, asceticism and courtesy. Now, by an inward ripening, the mind, after having been so long conversant with the forms of Antiquity, began to grasp its spirit. The incomparable simpleness and purity of the ancient culture, its exactitude of conception and of expression, its easy and natural thought and strong interest in men and in life, — all this began to dawn upon men's minds. Europe, after having lived in the shadow of Antiquity, lived in its sunshine once more.

This process of assimilation of the classic spirit, however, was intricate and full of incongruities. The new form and the new spirit do not yet coincide. The classical form may serve to express the old conceptions: more than one humanist chooses the sapphic strophe for a pious poem of purely medieval inspiration. Traditional forms, on the other hand, may contain the spirit of the coming age. Nothing is more erroneous than to identify classicism and modern culture.

The fifteenth century in France and the Netherlands is still medieval at heart. The diapason of life had not yet changed. Scholastic thought, with symbolism and strong formalism, the thoroughly dualistic conception of life and the world still dominated. The two poles of the mind continued to be chivalry and hierarchy. Profound pessimism spread a general gloom over life. The gothic principle prevailed in art. But all these forms and modes were on the wane. A high and strong culture is declining, but at the same time and in the same sphere new things are being born. The tide is turning, the tone of life is about to change.

THE INTERPRETATION OF THE RENAISSANCE: SUGGESTIONS FOR A SYNTHESIS

WALLACE K. FERGUSON

One cannot think of the "problem of the Renaissance" without the name of Wallace K. Ferguson coming to mind. Formerly at New York University and now Professor of History at the University of Western Ontario, Dr. Ferguson is well known for his writings on the Renaissance and especially for his fundamental work, *The Renaissance in Historical Thought.*

THE ATTEMPT to find an historical interpretation of the Renaissance, or of any other age, is predicated upon the acceptance of certain methodological assumptions. We must assume first the value of periodization and of synthesis, and the possibility of achieving both in a significant way. Few historians would now deny the value of periodization, though there are some who would still argue that the historian's task consists simply in recounting events as they occurred. But, in fact, periodization is an intellectual tool, essential to the historian's trade. Its use, to quote Collingwood's dictum, "is a mark of advanced and mature historical thought, not afraid to interpret facts instead of merely ascertaining them." Whether his periods be decades, centuries, or larger chronological areas such as the Middle Ages or the Renaissance, the historian cannot think about history without them, much less interpret it for others. There is perhaps less agreement concerning the need for synthesis, particularly among scholars who are concerned primarily with one discipline or one aspect of history. Yet even for specialists, some general notion of the character of the age they deal with, and of the relation of their own field of interest

to the total complex of its civilization, seems to me essential. Without some such general conception, the specialist may well find himself operating in an historical vacuum, in which the gravity of all objects seems equal.

A synthetic interpretation, which includes all aspects of a given civilization, is especially important for its bearing upon the problem of causation, even in the most restricted fields of enquiry. Painting, sculpture, music, poetry, science, philosophy, or theology may each develop to a certain extent along lines dictated by the discipline itself, either by a kind of inner logic, or as the result of the contribution of individual men of genius. Yet the general direction taken by any one of these can never, I believe, be fully understood or explained without consideration of other contemporaneous or antecedent changes in economic activity, political institutions, social configurations, and religious beliefs, or in these more imponderable shifts in ways of thinking which we classify under the heading of climates of opinion, or which we designate, such being the poverty of the English language, as the *Zeitgeist,* or the *Weltanschauung* of the age. The interrelation of these various

From Wallace K. Ferguson, "The Interpretation of the Renaissance: Suggestions for a Synthesis," in the *Journal of the History of Ideas,* XII (1951), 483–495. By permission of the editors of the *Journal of the History of Ideas.*

forms of historical activity may be difficult to establish with certainty; but the scholar who ignores the possibility of a causal relation between them and the subject of his own special interest, or who is content to recount *what* occurred without venturing to suggest *why* it may have occurred, is, I think, using the concept of scientific objectivity as a pretext for avoiding the necessity of thought.

But, if we admit the value of periodization and the desirability of synthesis, can these be applied satisfactorily to the concept of the Renaissance? In many disciplines, especially the history of art and music, the term Renaissance has been commonly used as a style concept, as distinguished, for example, from Late Gothic or Baroque. In other fields, notably the history of literature and the history of ideas, it has been used to designate a movement of thought, something which may influence, coincide with, or run counter to, such contemporaneous movements as the Reformation. Such uses of the term, if consciously defined, are justified within the framework of the particular discipline, and in both instances there is an implicit periodization, since certain chronological limits are assumed. For purposes of synthesis, however, the term Renaissance should, I think, be given a broader and more specifically periodic connotation, and be applied to the entire civilization of the age. It is as a period in the history of Western civilization, then, that I shall discuss it. Nor shall I pause here to justify the use of the term in this connotation, unfortunate though it is in many respects. I suspect it is here to stay. There is, in any case, little to be gained by re-enacting the miracle of the confusion of terms. The real problem is not what the age should be called, but what were its most characteristic traits and its chronological boundaries. How, in short, can we establish a periodic concept of the Renaissance that will prove a useful tool for the historian, and have practical value for the interpretation of history?

It would seem, at first glance, that the primary problem in periodization is to establish the chronological limits of the period in question. But that cannot be done without first forming some idea of what are the characteristics that distinguish it from the preceding and following ages. To serve the purpose of historical thought, a period must possess for the historian some conceptual content. It must correspond to a significant stage in the development of a civilization or a part thereof. Otherwise it is merely an arbitrarily selected and meaningless section of time. But significant periods do not emerge of themselves out of the unbroken flow of historical activity as it occurred from day to day and from year to year. It is the task of the thoughtful historian to discern, by close study of the facts, noteworthy changes in the course of history; and this he cannot do without at the same time forming a concept of the nature of these changes. Having determined to his own satisfaction what are the fundamental characteristics of a particular stage in historical development, he may then determine more exactly the chronological limits of the period to which these characteristics apply. This process should not be regarded as the imposition upon historical reality of an arbitrary scheme, founded upon *a priori* reasoning. All that is meant is that in the interpretation of history, as in the study of the natural sciences, an hypothesis must arise out of observation, if the infinitude of isolated facts is to be arranged in some coherent pattern and so be made accessible to thought.

To return to the problem of the Renaissance, the first step in establishing a period that will have practical value for the historian must be to form, from the infinite variety of available fact, an hypothesis concerning its essential character. Divergence of opinion in this respect is, indeed, the principal cause of the bewildering diversity of opinion regarding the chronological scope of the Renaissance. When the Italian Renaissance first emerged, like Pallas Athene, full-grown from the head of Jacob Burckhardt, it possessed certain traits that were regarded as characteristic of Italian culture during the whole period from Dante to the Counter-Reformation. Of these traits, individualism was, in Burckhardt's synthesis, the determining factor. He regarded this as primarily the product of the unique social and political organization which had shaped the genius of the Italian people, but he also attributed it in secondary degree to the revival of the classics. The influence of the latter, he thought, was predominant in the most characteristic forms of Renaissance literature and art, and also gave rise to the pagan spirit that was commonly regarded as an essential element of Renaissance culture. The periodic concept of the Renaissance thus continued to be attached, more or less, as was the older and narrower conception of the *renaissance des lettres,* to the revival of antiquity. When northern scholars strove to establish a Renaissance period for their own countries, they found that equivalent phenomena occurred much later than in Italy, and largely as importations. They thought of the Renaissance as having crossed the Alps at some time around the middle or end of the fifteenth century. The chronological beginnings of the Renaissance thus varied from country to country by a century or more. Still other scholars, reacting against the significance traditionally assigned to the revival of antiquity, thrust the beginnings of the Renaissance back to St. Francis, or continued the Middle Ages through to the Elizabethans. And some, particularly the historians of the natural sciences, regarding humanist culture with a bilious eye, looked before and after and pined for what was not, with the result that for them the Renaissance disappeared entirely, or became at best a kind of Middle Age, a regrettable lapse of time between two great periods of scientific thought.

Much of this chronological confusion arose, it seems to me, from constructing the concept of the Renaissance upon too narrow a foundation. If we take into consideration the total complex of European civilization, it will become evident, I think, that all the countries of Western Europe entered upon a period of decisive change about the beginning of the fourteenth century. The character as well as the rate of change varied from country to country, and from one type of culture, or institution, or form of activity, to another. But wherever we look, the typically medieval forms begin to disintegrate, while new and recognizably modern forms appear, if only in embryo. At the same time the centre of gravity shifts noticeably from the social and cultural factors that had been dominant in the Middle Ages to those minority phenomena that were to assume a leading role in the modern period. To define the Renaissance in a sentence seems rather like rushing in where not only angels but even fools would fear to tread. To avoid doing so at this point, however, would savor of moral cowardice. Viewing the Renaissance as an age in the history of Western Europe, then, I would define it as the age of transition from medieval to modern civilization, a period characterized primarily by the gradual shift from one fairly well coordinated and clearly defined type of civilization to another, yet, at the same time, possessing in its own right certain distinctive traits and a high degree of cultural vitality. And on the basis of this concept or hypothesis, I would set the arbitrary dates — 1300 to 1600 — as its chronological boundaries. To invest this definition with any significant content, however, and to pin down the weasel words, it is necessary, first of all, to indicate what may be considered the prevailing elements of both medieval and modern civilization, and then to trace the main lines of development within the transitional period.

In the broadest terms, then: the two dominant institutions of the Middle Ages were the feudal system and the universal church. Between them, they determined both the social structure and the ideological content of medieval civilization. And both, in their institutional aspects, were founded upon an agrarian, land-holding economy. Feudalism, indeed, took shape in the early Middle Ages very largely because it was the only possible means of maintaining social and political organization in a moneyless economy —

an economy in which the land and its produce were almost the sole form of wealth — commerce, industry and normal city life having virtually disappeared. Lacking financial resources in fluid form, central government was unable to maintain effective political or judicial authority, and was forced to relinquish these into the hands of the great land-holders. Lay society was divided into two hereditary classes of widely divergent status: the land-holding nobility, whose duty it was to fight and govern; and the peasants, more or less servile, whose duty it was to work the land. Only one other class had a useful service to perform: the clergy, whose duty it was to pray and to care for the souls of men. Having no other means of support, the clergy necessarily became a land-holding class, and, as land-holders, the officers of the church became feudal lords. On the material side, then, the church was deeply involved in the feudal system. At the same time, the church had inherited from its origins in the Roman Empire a principle of universality and a centralized, hierarchical government, which it never lost. But this universal authority was of too large a sort to come into direct conflict with the highly localized government of the feudal nobles. Feudalism and the universal church, indeed, could live more or less harmoniously together as *concordantia oppositorum*.

Into this agrarian, feudal society the commercial revival of the eleventh and twelfth centuries introduced the new and alien elements of commerce and skilled industry, with the resulting growth of cities and the expansion of money economy. This was followed by a notable increase in the prosperity and the fluid wealth of the land-holding classes. It was also accompanied by a great quickening of cultural activity, by that full development of clerical and feudal culture that made the twelfth and thirteenth centuries the classic period of medieval civilization. The economic stimulus which spread from the growing cities, together with the heightened tempo of intercommunication along the lines of trade,

was I think, the material factor that made possible the immense cultural vitality of these two centuries. But the content and spirit of that culture did not emanate from the urban classes. Learning remained the exclusive monopoly of the clergy. Art and music served the church. And vernacular literature expressed the ideals of feudalism and chivalry. Exceptions to these broad statements will, of course, leap to mind immediately. It is my contention, merely, that the elements of medieval civilization which I have mentioned were the most general, and the most characteristic.

When we turn to the modern age, say by the beginning of the seventeenth century, the general complex of European civilization has changed so radically that it amounts to a change in kind rather than in degree. The economic balance has shifted from agriculture to commerce and industry. Money economy has become almost universal, and capitalism has replaced all but the vestigial remnants of medieval economic organization. On the political side, the national states with centralized government have taken the place of feudal particularism, while at the same time the unity of Christendom has been decisively broken. Beside the Catholic Church stand the Protestant churches and sects, in their infinite variety. The social balance has shifted, so that the urban classes are no longer a minor element in society, but are prepared to assume political and cultural leadership. The clerical monopoly of learning has been broken, and laymen have replaced the clergy as the most numerous and influential group, both as patrons and creators of the higher forms of culture. The secular elements in literature, learning and general *Weltanschauung* now decisively outweigh the transcendental; and the natural sciences have replaced theology as the dominant form of knowledge.

Compared with the revolutionary changes in the character of Western European civilization between the years 1300 and 1600, the changes in the following three centuries are changes in degree rather than in kind.

Despite the increasingly rapid tempo of development, the evolution of modern civilization has followed, or did follow at least until our generation, lines already clearly established by the beginning of the seventeenth century. It is my contention, then, that medieval and modern civilization, despite the common elements that have remained constant in the Western world for the past two thousand years or more, are, in effect, two different types of civilization, and that the change from the one to the other occurred during the three centuries of the Renaissance.

But, in thus asserting the transitional character of the Renaissance, I have done no more than lay the ground work for an interpretation of the age itself. The mere characterization of the types of civilization that preceded and followed it suggests the lines of change within the transitional age, but does nothing to indicate how or why the changes took place. Here we must face the fundamental problem of causation. What were the dynamic forces that disintegrated the medieval social structure, and as a result altered medieval ways of thinking, gradually at first, but in the long run so profoundly as to create a new type of culture? In thus framing the question, I am, of course, implying a partial answer to the problem of causation, for there is implied in the question the assumption that the fundamental causes of change in the forms of culture are to be found in antecedent changes in economic and political institutions and in the whole structure of society. This is an assumption that many scholars, notably those imbued with the traditions of Hegelian or Thomist idealism, would be loath to accept. Yet it seems to me that, if we regard the whole complex of European civilization in this period, social change everywhere precedes cultural change, and that what is new in Renaissance culture, including novel adaptations of inherited traditions, can most readily be explained as the product of a changed social milieu.

Let me repeat my earlier generalization — that medieval culture was predominantly feudal and ecclesiastical, the product of a society founded upon an agrarian, land-holding economy. By the beginning of the fourteenth century that society had already been replaced in Italy by an urban society, constructed upon an economic foundation of large-scale commerce and industry, and with rapidly developing capitalist institutions. In the northern countries the expansion of money economy worked more slowly, but by 1300 it was already disintegrating the land-holding basis of feudal society, and had at the same time made possible the effective exercise of central government in the great national or territorial states. Both politically and economically, the feudal nobles were losing ground to the rising forces of monarchy and the bourgeoisie. Meanwhile the church was also entering upon a period of profound crisis when, with its moral prestige sapped by a monetary fiscal policy, it was forced into a losing battle with the newly arisen political power of the national states. Though it survived as a universal church for about a century after the Council of Constance, it never recovered the prestige and authority lost during the period of the Babylonian Captivity and the Great Schism.

The changes in the social structure and in the balance of the social classes, which resulted from these economic and political developments, were not reflected immediately or in equal degree everywhere by changes in the forms of higher culture. But, with due allowance for a normal cultural lag, it seems to me that as the economic, political, and social balance shifted, the leadership in all forms of intellectual and aesthetic activity also shifted in the same directions: from the clergy to the laity, from the feudal classes to the urban, and from the isolation of monastic foundations and baronial castles to the concentrated society of cities and of royal or princely courts.

One of the ways in which the influence of economic and political change worked most directly upon Renaissance culture was through the spread of lay education and lay patronage of art, learning, and letters. And this, I think, was clearly the result of the massing of population in cities, of the growth of large private fortunes, and of the concentration of both fluid wealth and political power in the hands of kings and princes. Under the conditions of feudal life, the noble classes made no pretence to intellectual eminence or scholarship sublime, and as Professor Pollard once remarked, even today a little thinking goes a long way in rural England. Not only did ideas circulate more rapidly in an urban atmosphere, but capitalist enterprise necessitated a general literacy among the middle and upper classes of the cities, while at the same time it furnished the most prosperous of the urban patriciate with the means for liberal patronage. In similar fashion, the growth of centralized state governments, supported by taxation, opened up careers to laymen trained in law and administration, and also created new centres of lay patronage. The princely courts of Italy all became active centres of lay culture, and had also, incidentally, broken completely with the feudal traditions that had inspired the greater part of lay culture in the Middle Ages. The royal courts of the North, and semi-royal courts like that of the Dukes of Burgundy, retained the forms of a feudal and chivalrous society, but the literary reflections of these forms had by the fifteenth century lost the vitality that had inspired the feudal literature of the twelfth and thirteenth centuries. The forms of feudalism and chivalry no longer bore a close relation to social reality. Economic and political pressure combined to transform the semi-independent baron of the Middle Ages into the Renaissance courtier. The ranks of the nobility were being infiltrated by the *nouveau riche,* and beside the remnants of the old *noblesse d'épée* now stood the wealthy and highly cultured members of the *noblesse de la robe.* To maintain their position at court, scions of the old nobility were being forced to don a veneer of education and cultured taste, and to extend their intellectual interests beyond the spheres of courtly love and refined homicide which had been the principal

themes of medieval feudal literature. The spread of lay education among the upper ranks of both the bourgeoisie and the nobility thus served not only to break the ecclesiastical monopoly of learning and the patronage of art, but also to modify radically the feudal and chivalrous spirit of vernacular literature. As higher education was adapted increasingly to the needs of a lay society, even the clergy were exposed more than ever before to secular learning, so that their contribution to Renaissance culture was in many instances indistinguishable from that of the educated layman.

The increasing laicization of education and of learning, literature, art and music was accompanied, almost inevitably, by an expansion of their secular content, and frequently by the introduction of a more secular tone. By this I do not mean to imply that the men of the Renaissance were, in general, less religious than those of the Middle Ages. There has been enough nonsense written about the pagan spirit of the Renaissance without my adding to it. On the other hand, it seems to me equally nonsensical to seize upon every evidence of religious feeling or belief in the Renaissance as proof that its culture was still basically medieval. Christianity was not a medieval invention. The Christian tradition certainly continued from the Middle Ages through the Renaissance — and beyond — but it did not continue unaltered, nor did it in the same degree dominate the culture of the age. In the first place, the greatly increased participation of laymen introduced into learning, literature and art whole areas of secular knowledge and subjects of general human interest which, if not wholly lacking in the Middle Ages, were yet inadequately represented. In the second place, the writer or artist, who worked for a predominantly lay audience or for lay patrons, had to meet the demands and satisfy the taste of men not trained in theology nor bound by clerical traditions. Even the religious art of the Renaissance gives frequent evidence of consideration for the taste of lay patrons. Finally, religion itself was in some degree laicized. This is evident, in the fourteenth and fifteenth centuries, in the growth of anti-clerical sentiment, and in revolts against the hierarchical authority of the church and the sacramental-sacerdotal aspects of medieval religion. The Wycliffite and Hussite heresies are extreme cases. But even within the bounds of orthodoxy, such movements of popular mysticism as the *Devotio Moderna* in the Netherlands show a tendency toward the development of a peculiarly lay piety. The religious writing of the Christian humanists offers further examples of an increasingly independent participation of laymen in the shaping of religious thought. These men were deeply pious, but they had little in common with Thomas Aquinas or Innocent III. The Protestant Reformation itself was in part a revolt against the sacerdotal domination of religion. In proclaiming the priesthood of all believers, Luther placed the believing layman on an even footing with the cleric. The whole problem of the relation of the Reformation to both medieval and Renaissance culture is, however, too complex to be discussed here. For the present, I can do no more than assert the opinion that it can be fully understood only if it is considered in relation to the changes that had altered the whole structure of European society and the character of European culture since the beginning of the fourteenth century. In short, I think that the Reformation must be interpreted as one aspect of Renaissance civilization, rather than as something running counter to it.

The emphasis I have placed upon social and cultural change, upon the decline of medieval and the rise of modern elements, is in accordance with my conception of the Renaissance as a transitional age. But, as I defined it, the Renaissance was also an age which possessed, aside from the uneasy coexistence within it of medieval and modern characteristics, certain distinctive traits and a high degree of cultural vitality. Here I can do no more than suggest answers to a few of the innumerable questions posed by this latter aspect of the problem. In the first place, whence came the cultural vitality of the Renaissance? Having no time for any but the briefest and most dogmatic of statements, I would say that it was made possible by unprecedented wealth and by the participation of an unprecedented variety of social types. I would say, further, that it drew its positive inspiration from the intellectual excitement caused by the challenge of new conditions of life, of new potentialities in every field of culture, and, in general, of a sense of breaking new ground and of scanning ever-widening horizons. Within the civilization of the Renaissance there were, of course, innumerable cross-currents, inconsistencies, and apparent reactions. These, I think, were the natural results of the conflict, more intense in this age than in any other since the dawn of Christianity, between inherited tradition and a changing society. The Renaissance was an age of moral, religious, intellectual and aesthetic crisis. This has been recognized often enough. What has not always been so clearly recognized in this connection is that it was also an age of acute crisis in economic, political and social life.

In the second place, was the Renaissance an age marked to a peculiar degree by the spirit of individualism? This is a difficult question to answer, for individualism is a perilously protean concept. It is also more than a little shop-worn, and it bears the marks of much careless handling. In any case, I find it difficult to think in terms of *the spirit* of the Renaissance, just as I find it impossible to envisage *the Renaissance man*. Such a complex and vital age must have had many spirits, good and bad, though probably few indifferent. Nevertheless, it does seem to me that there was in this transitional age a growing awareness of personality and a keener sense of individual autonomy than had been possible in the social and cultural conditions of the Middle Ages; and it may be that this trait was more strongly marked, more aggressive, in the Renaissance than in later ages, when the individual's right to self-determination was more easily taken for granted. To individualism, thus defined, many factors contributed, in addition to those mentioned by Burckhardt; for there were more changes in the heaven and earth of Renaissance men than were dreamed of in Burckhardt's philosophy — for example, the growth of a lay piety that stressed the individual man's direct communion with God, and, at the other end of the moral spectrum, the development of a capitalist spirit that stressed the individual man's direct communion with Mammon. With the dislocation of European society that accompanied the breaking up of medieval institutions, men were left more dependent than before upon their own personal qualities, while the increasing complexity of social organization opened up a wider choice of careers, and more varied opportunities for the development of personal tastes and interests.

Finally, what is the role in the Renaissance of the revival of antiquity? That I have left discussion of the classical revival to the last does not mean that I regard it as unimportant. Rather the reverse. But I do think that its causative force, great though it was, was of a secondary character; that, indeed, the enthusiasm with which classical literature and learning were seized upon was itself caused by antecedent changes in the social structure, which became effective first in Italy, and later in the North. That men should love the classics, once exposed to them, has always seemed to classicists an obvious fact needing no explanation. Yet I think that the intense, almost excessive enthusiasm for classical culture, which was peculiar to the Renaissance, can be explained only by the fact that it was perfectly designed to meet the needs of educated, urban laymen, of a society that had ceased to be predominantly either feudal or ecclesiastical, yet had in its own immediate past nothing to draw upon for inspiration but the feudal and ecclesiastical traditions of the Middle Ages. I am not forgetting that the twelfth century also had its clerical humanists, notably John of Salisbury, but their humanism was of a different

sort, and between them and Petrarch fell the shadow of scholasticism. The humanism of the Renaissance was not a clerical humanism, though there were clerical humanists — and it was certainly not feudal. It cut across the most characteristic of medieval traditions. When the mania for antiquity had passed its peak, and the writers of the sixteenth century were laying the foundations for the modern national literatures, they wrote not only for one class but for all cultured people.

Without minimizing the importance of the revival of antiquity, it is also worth noting that, even where the classics exerted no direct influence, as in music, the Renaissance broke new ground, and exhibited enormous vitality. This was the age that witnessed the greatest strides in the development of polyphony and the work of a long line of brilliant composers, from Machaut to Palestrina. Here, as in so many other aspects of Renaissance culture, the increasing participation of laymen, and the growth of lay patronage, was accompanied by the development of new forms and by the introduction of a larger proportion of secular content and tone. Music in the Renaissance was a social art, and a fair mastery of its techniques was an essential qualification for the successful courtier or indeed for any cultured person. Any account of sixteenth century social life leaves the impression that wherever two or three were gathered together they sang four or five part polyphony. I make no apology for thus ending my discussion of the Renaissance on a musical note. That any synthesis should leave an adequate place for music is, indeed, a point that I wish to emphasize; for it is one of the peculiarities of the traditional schools of *Kulturgeschichte* that, while giving full consideration to all the pictorial arts, they have scarcely afforded a passing word for music, the most closely related of all the arts to the life of the people.

In conclusion, may I disclaim any pretension to having solved all the problems of the Renaissance. The interpretation I have suggested is no more than a framework, within which there is room for much variation in treating the individual aspects of Renaissance civilization. Yet I feel that to approach the problems presented by the history of intellectual and aesthetic disciplines, of morality and religion, as well as of economic, political and social institutions from the point of view I have suggested will lead to a clearer understanding of the relation of each of these to the others and to the main currents of historical development. There is implied in this point of view a theory of historical interpretation, but not historical determinism. I would maintain, for example, that the growth of a wealthy urban society might well be regarded as a necessary conditioning factor in the development of Quattrocento art, whereas I find it difficult to see how the development of the art of the Quattrocento could have been a necessary conditioning factor in the growth of a wealthy urban society. Yet, I also see no reason to believe that such a society must necessarily have produced Donatello or Ghirlandajo. To say that things happened thus does not imply

that they could not have happened otherwise. In seeking to discover the causes of cultural phenomena, the historian must often be content with permissive or partially effective causes. He may be able to assert with some confidence what made a specific development possible, or even what determined its general direction, and what were the boundaries beyond which it could not go. But within that frame-work, he must always leave room for the unpredictable activity of the human spirit. He may be able to explain why the achievements of Michelangelo or Machiavelli, of Josquin des Prés or Erasmus were possible and why they would have been impossible a hundred years earlier or later, but what in these men was peculiar and personal eludes him. Realization of the fact that he cannot hope to explain everything fully, that history is not an exact science, should not, however, cause the historian to lose confidence in his craft or cease his endeavor to understand what can be understood. The historian's reach must exceed his grasp, or what's the study of history for?

MOOT PROBLEMS OF RENAISSANCE INTERPRETATION: AN ANSWER TO WALLACE K. FERGUSON

HANS BARON

Known as a supporter, with modifications, of many of Burckhardt's original theses, Dr. Baron was honored by having a special session of the American Historical Association meeting of December 1956 devoted to an examination of his contributions to the study of the Renaissance—an honor seldom accorded a living scholar. Part of his paper given on this occasion follows.

ACCORDING to the "Conclusion" of Ferguson's *Renaissance in Historical Thought,* the bracket that we need most as a complement to the other fields considered for Renaissance interpretation is the economic history of the Renaissance; and nobody can contest the justification of this contention. But how achieve such fusion today in the practice of historical work? Among economic historians, there is a consensus at present that so far as the economic activities of the Italian merchant class are concerned, "Renaissance individualism" had already reached its zenith by about 1300, if not earlier, and that during the period called by the cultural historian "The Renaissance," the trade volume, the population figures, and even, as many economic students contend, the merchant's enterprising spirit, as well as his public-mindedness, had become inferior to what they had been in the preceding centuries. These facts and inferences, if they constitute the whole of the truth, may lead one to argue that according to the teachings of economic history the true age that deserves the name of "Renaissance"

is the thirteenth century, and this is what leading economic historians have been proclaiming, from J. Strieder's paper on "Origin and Evolution of Early European Capitalism," thirty years ago, to the present veritable crusade of A. Sapori in favor of a reassignment of the term "Renaissance" to thirteenth-century Italy. We may ask: would we obtain an intelligible picture, or would we come nearer to the truth, if we were to conclude that after "The Renaissance" had flowered and was already withering in economic life, "the Renaissance" began to start in Humanism, philosophy, and literature? And that the citizens of Florence, as humanists, proclaiming that there could be no true culture withdrawn from the life of the community, at the same time when as merchants they decided that the prudent man should keep aloof from public burdens and honors?

To my mind, the cause of this confusion lies in the circumstance that our present notion of "economic individualism," which is invariably placed parallel to the Burckhardtian concept of Renaissance individual-

From Hans Baron, "Moot Problems of Renaissance Interpretation: An Answer to Wallace K. Ferguson," in the *Journal of the History of Ideas,* XIX (1958), 31–34. By permission of the editors of the *Journal of the History of Ideas.*

ism, has not yet been sufficiently put through the filter of modern criticism; there have been different kinds of "individualism," and not every phase and group of the Quattrocento and Cinquecento was characterized by lack of the public spirit. If the recent political and cultural reappraisal of the horizon and conduct of the Florentine aristocracy and intellectual class during the early Quattrocento proves correct, the day will come when economic students of the same period will feel compelled to loosen their still too uniform and rigid notion of *"the* merchant of the Renaissance" and elaborate, more distinctly than has been done until today, a variety of types and groups, among which the Florentine *Lana* industrialist, the chief upholder of the new politics and culture of the period, can take a place of his own beside the pure "economic man" Francesco Datini, creature of provincial Prato and cosmopolitan Avignon, who today is almost generally looked upon as the true paradigm of the Florentine-Tuscan merchant about 1400. But unless and until such changes in the frame of reference among economic students take place, the best advice for the historian of the humanistic Renaissance would seem to be to go on with the specific promising approach now available to him and frankly admit that at this moment not every cultivated area of Renaissance research can receive an adequate share in a coherent interpretation of the civilization of the Renaissance.

With this enforced limitation, our situation is, after all, not different from that of our predecessors. For in the past, as Ferguson's penetrating book on the history of Renaissance interpretations has shown so persuasively, the greatest increments in the historical understanding of the Renaissance were always due not to rounded and comprehensive portraits of the period but rather to successive fresh approaches, entered upon now in one, now in another field, as new perspective opened up from varying vantage points that became accessible with the changes of interests and experiences

during the century from Burckhardt to the present.

I say: from Burckhardt, because it would be a mistake to think that Burckhardt produced any "synthesis" different not only in quality but in structure from the "perspective" and "reinterpretations" which followed. If by the word "synthesis" we mean a total picture whose strength lies in a systematic collection and balanced composition of all available approaches and data, few important historical books, indeed, deserve the name "synthesis" as little as Burckhardt's "Essay" (as he called his book deliberately). From the late eighteenth century, Italian scholars had described as a coherent period the time from the acquisition of autonomy by the Communes in the eleventh century, to Tyranny, Patronage, and Humanism about 1500. Hume, in England, and later Sismondi, in Geneva, had traced the flowering of that period to the effects of freedom in competition which existed among the citizens of the city-republics and, in the fifteenth century, among the members of a system of independent states. From this older, much more comprehensive synthesis Burckhardt annexed for his purposes the fourteenth and fifteenth centuries alone, and there he focussed his attention on one objective: to determine the factors which in the republics as well as in the tyrannies helped to dissolve the public civic spirit and mold that ruthless individualism in which he saw the source of greatness as well as the guilt of the age. Yet it was precisely by this contraction of focus, and this restriction of the material to a period freshly intelligible to him in its mind and sentiments, that he succeeded in creating a new vista. Writing in the mid-nineteenth century, when contemporary culture was keenly individualistic and had a strong aesthetic note, he could discern in Renaissance Italy the prototype and exemplar of these modern attitudes. The greatness of his work, indeed, derived from his power to establish the traits which he was first to note so permanently and with so lavish a mass of sources that *Die Kultur der Renaissance in Italien* will remain *the* introduction to the Renaissance as far as the Renaissance was an age of individualism.

Today, a hundred years after Burckhardt — so I would argue — culture, as well as opinions as to the value of Humanism for our own world, have so profoundly changed that for the first time the limitations of the Burckhardtian pattern of reference can be fully grasped, although his fundamental discovery, that Renaissance Italy somehow was a prototype of the modern world, has preserved its truth. Now that the relations between culture, society, and citizenship have become keen problems for us, we can discern that the humanistic education and philosophy of life, in many interesting respects, represent a first approach to our own problems and solutions; just as we are now beginning to recognize that the modern struggle against the dangers of classicism was not entirely unknown before the eighteenth century, but to a degree inherent in Renaissance Humanism from its Quattrocento stage.

Even though a comprehensive counterpart to Burckhardt's *Kultur der Renaissance* has not appeared as yet and may never appear, the years since the end of World War II have seen these and similar observations spread in an increasingly larger body of studies. If we expect their final results to be as peripheral as Thode's and Walser's proof that older forms of piety left their marks on Renaissance culture, a more promising approach may, indeed, be a "synthesis" which, by taking something from all approaches, past and present, might erect an edifice much richer than that now outmoded shell in which Burckhardt clothed his discovery of Renaissance individualism. But if we assume, as many scholars now do, that today we are witnessing the emergence of an incisive reinterpretation from the vantage point of the scholarship of our own age, such essential reappraisal will offer the best prospect for the future.

SUGGESTIONS FOR ADDITIONAL READING

The historiography of the problem of the Renaissance is very complex and the literature on the varying concepts of the Renaissance is very extensive. It is thus fortunate that there is available an excellent survey of the literature in Wallace K. Ferguson's *The Renaissance in Historical Thought: Five Centuries of Interpretation* (Boston, 1948). This work is a comprehensive and detailed study of the concept of the Renaissance as it existed in the minds of the writers of various epochs beginning with the Italian humanists themselves. Burckhardt's outstanding essay is discussed in Chapter VII and the remaining half of the work is devoted to an analysis of the more recent writings on the subject of the Renaissance and how they support, modify, or disagree with Burckhardt's synthesis. Bibliographical surveys of the literature dealing with the Renaissance can also be found in H. Schulte Nordholt, *Het Beeld der Renaissance: Een Historiografische Studie* (Amsterdam, 1948) and in Herman Baeyens, *Begrip en Probleem van de Renaissance* (Louvain, 1952).

Jacob Burckhardt's work, *The Civilization of the Renaissance in Italy,* should be read in its entirety. Only in this way can this masterful essay be truly appreciated. A number of English editions are available, but it must be noted that in many editions the text and notes have been augmented by another German historian. The edition of 1944 (Phaidon Press) in the translation of S. G. C. Middlemore is recommended not only because it contains the original text but also because of the hundred plates appended to this volume.

At first, indeed for half a century, historians were content to follow Burckhardt in general, only amplifying details or remodeling them slightly as specialized studies increased the depth of knowledge of the period of the Renaissance. John Addington Symonds expanded Burckhardt's essay into a well-written seven-volume general study, *Renaissance in Italy* (London, 1875–86). Pasquali Villari, in a patriotic vein, popularized the period in his *Life and Times of Girolamo Savonarola,* 2 vols. (Eng. trans., London, 1888) and his *Life and Times of Niccolo Machiavelli* (Eng. trans., London, 1889). Volume I of the *Cambridge Modern History* (Cambridge, 1902) was also much influenced by the basic Burckhardt tradition.

Writers of intellectual, social, and economic history, soon examined in detail these areas slighted or ignored by Burckhardt. The intellectual history of the Renaissance was studied by Wilhelm Dilthey and Ernst Cassirer. The latter stressed the originality of the period in his *Individuum und Kosmos in der Philosophie der Renaissance* (Leipzig, 1927) and in his articles, "Giovanni Pico della Mirandola," *Journal of the History of Ideas,* III (1942) and "Some Remarks on the Question of the Originality of the Renaissance," *Ibid.,* IV (1943). Leonardo Olschki traced the development of scientific thought in the vernacular literature and the role in this development of the practical technician and artist. In a number of works Giovanni Gentile dealt with the growth of the scientific spirit, rising out of the humanistic opposition to scholasticism. Hans Baron, introduced to the reader in earlier pages, has long been engaged in showing the interrelations of ideas and the evolution of the social, political, and economic institutions of Renaissance Florence. Besides numerous German articles, the following may be read with profit: "The Historical Background of the Florentine Renaissance," *History,* N. Ser. XXII (1938); "A Sociological Interpretation of the Early Renaissance in Florence," *South Atlantic Quarterly* XXXVIII (1939); "Articulation and Unity in the Italian Renaissance," *Annual Report, American Historical Association,* III (1942).

The views of his articles can best be learned from his *Humanistic and Political Literature in Florence and Venice at the Beginning of the Quattrocento: Studies in Criticism and Chronology* (Cambridge, Mass., 1955) and his *The Crisis of the Early Italian Renaissance: Civic Humanism and Republican Liberty in an Age of Classicism and Tyranny,* 2 vols. (Princeton, 1955). Here the Burckhardtian thesis of a union of the "Revival of Antiquity" and the awakening of the Italian national spirit is stressed, with the latter being interpreted as Florentine in origin and character. Leonardo Bruni is his model for the new "civic humanism" which results from the crisis in Florentine history of the early Quattrocento.

In addition to the work of Alfred von Martin, the socio-economic explanation of Renaissance culture is also to be found in Edgar Zilsel's "The Sociological Roots of Science," *The American Journal of Sociology,* XLVII (1942) and in Ferdinand Schevill's *History of Florence from the Founding of the City through the Renaissance* (New York, 1936).

Also within the general Burckhardtian tradition, but contributing details and adding knowledge to the history of the literature and art of the Renaissance are Francesco de Santis' *Storia della letteratura italiana,* 2 vols. (Naples, 1870–71; Eng. trans. New York, 1931), Ludwig Geiger's *Renaissance und Humanismus in Italien und Deutschland* (Berlin, 1882), Philippe Monnier's *Le Quattrocento, Essai sur l'histoire littéraire du XVᵉ siècle italien,* 2 vols. (Paris, 1900, new ed. 1924), Eugène Muentz' *Histoire de l'art le Renaissance,* 3 vols. (Paris, 1889–95), and Max Dvořák's *Geschichte der italienischen Kunst im Zeitalter der Renaissance,* 2 vols. (Munich, 1927–28). E. Panofsky upholds the Renaissance as a style concept in his "Renaissance and Renascences," *Kenyon Review,* VI (1944).

The great amount of research in the late nineteenth and twentieth centuries, particularly in the history and civilization of the Middle Ages, was bound to produce modification and some opposition to the Burckhardtian thesis. Henry Thode considered St. Francis of Assisi as the moving spirit and inspiration of the Renaissance movement. In this he received support from the work of Emile Gebhart and Paul Sabatier. The contrast between the Middle Ages and the Renaissance which the Romanticists had maintained was rejected by Charles Homer Haskins in *The Renaissance of the Twelfth Century* (Cambridge, Mass., 1927) and in his *Studies in Medieval Culture* (Oxford, 1929). Friedrich von Bezold and Fedor Schneider wrote about the continuation of the classical tradition in medieval humanism, as did H. Liebeschutz in his *Mediaeval Humanism in the Life and Writings of John of Salisbury* (London, 1950) and E. K. Rand, "The Classics in the Thirteenth Century," *Speculum,* 1929). The role and influence of mystical lay piety in forming the Northern Renaissance was examined by Albert Hyma in his *The Christian Renaissance, a History of the "Devotio Moderna"* (New York, 1924). J. J. Walsh in his *The Thirteenth the Greatest of Centuries* (New York, 1907) claimed many modern elements could be found in the Age of Faith. Humanism was found even earlier by D. Knowles, "The Humanism of the Twelfth Century," *Studies: An Irish Quarterly Review,* XXX (1941).

James Westfall Thompson revealed the extent of medieval lay education in his work, *The Literacy of the Laity in the Middle Ages* (Berkeley, 1939). Douglas Bush pointed out the medievalism and the Christianity of Renaissance humanism in his *Mythology and the Renaissance Tradition in English Poetry* (Minneapolis, 1932) and in his *The Renaissance and English Humanism* (Toronto, 1939 and 1956). Roberto Weiss showed the strength of the medieval tradition in English humanism in his *Humanism in England during the Fifteenth Century* (Oxford, 1941).

Science is rightly considered as one of the most distinguishing elements of modern civilization, but the historians of science found much evidence of scientific achievement and speculation in the medieval period. The original studies of Pierre Duhem, *Le système du monde. Histoire des doctrines cosmologiques de Platon à Copernic,* 5 vols. (Paris, 1913–17) were continued and expanded by Lynn Thorndike, *A History of Magic and Experimental Sciences,* 6 vols. (New York, 1923–41) and *Science and Thought in the Fifteenth Century* (New York, 1929). George Sarton, who once wrote that "from a scientific point of view, the Renaissance was *not* a renaissance" in his "Science in the Renaissance" in J. W. Thompson, G. Rowley, *et al, The Civilization of the Renaissance* (Chicago, 1929), has greatly modified his earlier views in his recent *Six Wings: Men of Science in the Renaissance* (Bloomington, Ind., 1957). His monumental *Introduction to the History of Science,* 3 vols. in 5 (Baltimore, 1927–48) reflects his earlier views.

A large number of books and articles deal specifically with the problem of the Renaissance. Reviews of interpretive trends or studies of particular criteria can be found in R. H. Fife, "The Renaissance in the Changing World," *The Germanic Review,* IX (1939); E. F. Jacob, "The Fifteenth Century: Some Recent Interpretations," *Bulletin of the John Rylands Library,* XIV, (1930); N. Nelson, "Individualism as a Criterion of the Renaissance," *The Journal of English and Germanic Philology,* XXXII (1933); K. M. Setton, "Some Recent Views of the Renaissance," *Report of the Annual Meeting of the Canadian Historical Association* (1947); A. S. Turbeville and E. F. Jacob, "Changing Views of the Renaissance," *History,* N. S. XVI (1931–32); and W. W. J. Wilkinson, "The Meaning of the Renaissance," *Thought,* XVI (1941). The following four studies by H. Weisinger examine the theories of the Renaissance found in the writings of the humanists: "Renaissance Theories of the Revival of the Fine Arts," *Italica,* XX (1943); "The Self-Awareness of the Renaissance as a Criterion of the Renaissance," *Papers of the Michigan Academy of Science, Arts, and Literature,* XXIX (1944); "Who Began the Revival of Learning? The Renaissance Point of View," *Ibid.,* XXX (1944); "The Renaissance Theory of the Reaction against the Middle Ages as a Cause of the Renaissance," *Speculum,* XX (1945).

$$f(x) = \frac{x - h + x}{h}$$

$$= \frac{h}{h}$$